INDISH man

REFLECTIONS FROM
INDIA, BRITAIN AND THE SEA

GOPI CHANDROTH

TWAGAA
HTTPS://TWAGAA.COM

First published in 2025 by

TWAGAA
HTTPS://TWAGAA.COM

TWAGAA INTERNATIONAL
Mumbai (Maharashtra), India
Email: hello@twagaa.com
Website: https://twagaa.com

Cover Design by Sucharita Suri (sucharitas.world)
Book Typeset at Seek Red (seekred.com)

INDISHMAN - Reflections from India, Britain and the Sea
ISBN eBook: 978-81-991736-1-3
Paperback: 978-81-991736-4-4

10 9 8 7 6 5 4 3 2 1

Dedicated to the memory of my son

Aniruddh Gopinath

(1987-2009)

अयं निजः परो वेति गणना लघुचेतसाम् ।
उदारचरितानां तु वसुधैव कुटुम्बकम् ॥

The small-minded think this is mine and that is another's.
For the noble-hearted, the entire world is family.

~ *Mahā Upanisad (Book VI, verses 70–73)*

Contents

Preface

At an interview for the UK Civil Service, many years ago, a psychologist analysing my personality test results said to me, "Your profile is neither typically British nor Indian. What are you?"

"I am an Indishman," I would respond if I were asked this question today.

I am a product of diverse cultures, deeply influenced by the ancient value systems of India and the fine and gentle sensibilities of Britain. My sea career took me to faraway places and I was fortunate to visit almost every corner of the world. I like to believe that the widely varying ethos of the global family has made an impact on me. And that is reflected in these stories.

Over the years, I have realised that human beings are all very similar in their hopes and aspirations. Yet, it would be completely wrong to make generalisations about their character, nation, or community. Each of us is a unique individual with our own special, human stories. Man's worst enemy is perhaps his dogma.

When I talk about this book, the first question I am asked is: 'What is it about?'

I struggle to answer this because the book does not fit neatly into one genre. It comprises personal anecdotes, reflections, travel, a bit of street-philosophy and pure fiction. Fortunately, there are only seven pieces of fiction: 'The Elusive Reflection', 'Salsa Sally', 'Ambushed by a Book', 'Love 2050', 'No Return', 'Rory and Me' and the ending of 'The Last Light'. The rest are lived experiences. You may find that hard to believe – I do too, in retrospect. An ex-colleague at the Marine Accident Investigation Branch had once remarked that situations are specially set up to capture my reaction on a secret camera, as in the American TV show 'Candid Camera'. When I reminisce about the episodes that led to these stories, I begin to wonder if that is true.

Indishman does not have to be read in any particular order. Think of it as a jar of sweets. I sincerely hope you like some of them.

~

1

Eden of my Childhood

There is a place I cannot visit anymore except perhaps by writing about it.

Saturday morning – we set off in our black Hindustan on the 30-mile trip from Thalassery to Kunnoth. It is a weekly routine that spans from the beginning of my memory until I am nine. Father drives, mother sits in the front, a child or two squeezed in between them. My other siblings sit at the back, pulling my ears or occasionally pinching me just to pass the time.

We stop at Koothuparambu to visit my uncle, father's brother. The brothers tell each other little anecdotes, their trademark laughter sounds like they are having wheezing fits. Father's grey-green eyes twinkle in delight and his face reddens as the stuffed deer heads on the wall stare down at us indulgently. Their disproportionately large antlers mesmerise me with their elegant symmetry.

The yellow milestones on the side of the road, the seven white furlong markers within each mile, the verdant moss and blood-red hibiscus flash by as we resume our journey. Father stops the car after a few miles and gives a silver rupee to Bhaskaran, who waits by the roadside in expectation of his weekly gift. His lifeless limbs, afflicted by polio, are contorted in impossible directions. He smiles and waves goodbye, dragging himself off the tarmac.

The next stop is Mattannur, home of Kuttiraman, the child who spent his life in servitude to our family.

Kuttiraman was found standing at the gate when my brothers returned from school. This undernourished, semi-starved child, wearing only a red loincloth, was hired to look after me. I was almost the same size as him, although several years his junior. Kuttiraman grew up with us, finally emigrating to America and returning to Mattannur to become a mini-landowner himself. His story needs more telling, for his is also the story of the velvet revolution of Kerala, where the world's first Marxist government was democratically elected.

No American dream, though, for poor, crippled Bhaskaran. One Saturday, the last that I remember, a driver drives us to Kunnoth. Father is dozing, and Bhaskaran, having recognised our car, beams in expectation of his rupee, but the driver does not stop. I remember looking at him through the rear windscreen. His look of baffled disappointment still haunts me. The resentment of an entire people is distilled in his eyes. Why didn't I wake up father? Why do I still feel as if it was all my fault?

Onwards from Mattannur and across the bridge over the Iritty River. If you go there today, you will see a placid lake, the river having been dammed many years ago. But, to me, it is alive: a wild, galloping beast, furious, snorting iridescent sprays onto moss-laden banks, raging ahead in tumescent turbulence as giant, uprooted trees, like flotsam, cling to its deep, silver mane. We cross the bridge and leave the roiling river behind.

We arrive at Kunnoth and park our car by the stream that bisects our land: the stream where we catch tiny flame-coloured fish with a Kerala *thorthu* (a porous woven towel) and gently release them, the stream on the banks of which bushes of pineapple and sugarcane proudly flaunt their fecundity. In contrast, carpets of tremulous touch-me-nots close and withdraw when we trample them under our wellingtons.

Wellingtons are mandatory, even in the blazing hot summer. It is protection against venomous snakes. I see more of them in father's vivid descriptions and never really in flesh. But stories about snakes are sufficient to make us keep our boots on. We tread on dead leaves and abandoned ant hills without fear. We are told never to poke a stick into any hole in the ground or on earth mounds because even a newly hatched cobra could slither up the stick and kill us faster than we could withdraw the stick or drop it. Such is the fear of snakes that a harmless water snake frightened the hell out of us. But serpents are part of every story and our Eden was no different.

The tenants and labourers wait for father to pay their weekly wages. We slip away to cavort in the stream and climb smooth guava trees. We bite through the thick skin of sugarcane to relish its fibrous sweetness and finally return to the cool veranda of our thatched-roof house.

Banana leaves are placed on a ring of soft bark of the plantain tree, and ripe jackfruit leaves stitched into conical shapes with the spine of coconut fronds serve as spoons. Naranettan, manager and maître d', serves us hot rice gruel with delicious tapioca stew, whole black lentils, and a mélange of tender jackfruit with freshly grated coconut and spicy pickles. A dollop of ghee from the milk of our own cows, a couple of sweet little bananas, a piece of jaggery, and we are ready to go out again. Mother forces us to rest a while before we sneak out. All the used leaves and spoons are thrown into a huge compost pit behind the house. We rarely see or use plastic.

In the evening, father takes us along on his inspection of the farm. We are accompanied by a few tenants and Naranettan. People seek father's attention, invariably asking for his help in what seem to us as trivial matters. A woman needs a few rupees to buy a cow, someone wants to dig a small channel to divert water from our stream to their tenured land, someone else wants a piece of land to cultivate some grains. I cannot remember the details or if the decisions were in their favour, but I see most of them go away with a smile.

At dusk, father sits on an easy chair on the veranda, and tenants and others congregate in the compound below. The men stand, ever so slightly stooped, as a mark of supplicant respect, holding their customary thorthu turbans in their hands. The women stand to one side, whispering softly among themselves. Father, his socialist disposition in conflict with his feudal authority, speaks kindly to them, and I imagine metes out justice where required. He does not raise his voice at the tenants or even speak harshly to them. Or do we only remember what we want to, and forget the harsher moments? I narrate this as I remember. The concepts of feudalism and the inequities of disproportionate land ownership do not register in my six-year-old mind. But there is a restive unease that makes me slightly uncomfortable.

The weeks roll into months and years. Father shifts his law practice to the High Court in Kochi, and our visits to Kunnoth become infrequent. Naranettan leaves under a cloud and is replaced by Jaleel, the brave-heart who chopped a deadly king cobra in two with his machete as it stood on its tail hissing at him. Or so the story went.

Kerala enforces the Land Reforms Act, one of the two

Indian states that implements the federal Act. Most of our tenants became landowners. Kerala transforms from a poverty-stricken, caste-ridden plutocracy to a thriving, egalitarian, socialist state. The people of Kerala stand tall with their thorthus proudly crowning their heads.

On a journey from Thalassery to Bangalore, you will pass Kunnoth on your left just before your car starts climbing up the Western Ghats. If you recognise the Eden of my childhood, stop your car and peep inside. If nothing else, you will see the shy touch-me-nots. Touch them gently, on my behalf.

~

2

TLC

There is something about an unknown abbreviation that touches a nerve of insecurity in me. I am too inhibited to ask for the expansion just in case I am the only ignorant one in the room. But it is like encountering a missing rung on a ladder – it disconcerts and throws me off track.

My first accident investigation, back in 2007, was a fire that sank a yacht off the coast of Corsica. It was a private luxury yacht, carrying a family of twelve passengers and four crew. The fire that started in the fo'c'sle soon engulfed the entire vessel. The family escaped using the tender they had been towing. The skipper and crew tried unsuccessfully to extinguish the fire. Finally, they raised a Mayday call and jumped into the sea.

I interviewed the skipper on the phone a few days later. He narrated the events in minute detail, reliving his ordeal. He could not reconcile himself to the tragic loss of his vessel. The memory was still raw, causing him considerable distress. I could hear the tremor in his voice. I allowed a gentle pause to demonstrate my empathy, then continued the interview.

"So, you swam to the boat that responded to your Mayday call. Then what happened?"

"Yeah, they took us on board. Gave us dry clothes and blankets, and lots of TLC."

The abbreviation 'TLC' was not part of my lexicon. But I

dared not bare my ignorance by asking. However, my mind strayed. I only half listened to the skipper. I was stuck on TLC, and I knew this had to change. I did make an educated guess, but had to confirm. So, I interrupted his flow.

"What's TLC then? Some kind of sandwich?"

It sounded so much like BLT. Surely, it had to stand for tomato-lettuce-cucumber.

The skipper was too polite to laugh, but I could sense his smile through the phone. I was glad it was a telephone interview. My innocent expression would surely have cracked him up. He gave me the correct expansion. I could hear the lilt in his voice that told me I had lifted his spirits, even cheered him up a bit.

From that day on, I made a point of challenging every unfamiliar abbreviation. I no longer cared if people thought any less of me. I realised that in the business of saving lives, pride has no place. It was my first true epiphany in the profession. Accident investigation is like mathematics: if you don't understand every step, you are bound to lose the plot.

~

3

Heirlooms

An heirloom has no monetary value for its owner – until it's stolen or lost. If you find that assertion outrageous, do read on.

Let's assume you own a diamond necklace worth about £1 million. That's what it would cost to replace it today. You inherited it from your mother, who got it from her mother, who got it from ... you get the idea. It's been in the family for several generations. It's valuable not just in monetary terms but also in emotional value. It is an heirloom. So, you would never sell it. Not to buy that jazzy new car you've always craved, not to finance the house extension you dream of, not even to send your children to Harvard. OK, scrub Harvard – let's say MIT.

You hold on to it as if your life depends on it. You wouldn't part with it even if you were starving. Well, maybe if you were starving, but how many hungry diamond owners are there in this world?

What you guard with your life, what you lose sleep over, is in fact worthless – monetarily speaking. Sentimental value? Certainly. But you can't eat sentiment, nor can you exchange it for a new car. You might as well store a piece of granite in your high-security safe. Lose it, however, and suddenly its financial potential dazzles you with its brilliance, like the floodlights of a Premier League match – or like diamonds.

Let's explore this further. Imagine, one day, your diamond

necklace – God forbid – is stolen. You file an insurance claim. A cool million lands in your bank account, taking the sting out of your loss. Yes, you'll miss the heirloom. Your children will be deprived of their inheritance. But new money opens doors for you and your children. Loss metamorphoses into gain.

And the thief? He's laughing all the way to the bank. No sloppy sentiment for him, no emotional baggage, just unadulterated profit. With the proceeds, he might send his children to medical school, buy a yacht, retire to a Caribbean island. The potential is vast. The loss of an heirloom, then, improves life for two parties: you and the thief. Three in fact, if you include the bank – £2 million is not something even a bank would sniff at.

I should know. I wear one such heirloom every day: a watch that belonged to my father. It's over forty years old. I wear it everywhere, despite the risk of getting mugged – whether in the Bronx in New York or Maputo in Mozambique. I've swum in the sea and sweated in saunas with the watch on my wrist. It runs smoothly, uncomplaining, drawing energy from the movement of my arm. I take it off only when I sleep.

Recently, I took an overnight train from Bangalore to Thalassery, my hometown in Kerala. Within an hour of boarding, I was ruing my decision to travel by train. I couldn't recapture the magic of train journeys past. Too much had changed. No more fresh breeze on one's face from open windows, no clack-clack of wheels on rails, which, like a sweet lullaby, induce somnolence. Instead, the coach is an air-conditioned cold-box with tinted windows that obscure the view. The internal noise is almost unbearable as fellow passengers complain about their government, the quality of food, and cleanliness of toilets. Vendors march back and forth in the aisles repeatedly announcing their wares: samosas, cutlets, tea-coffee, biriyani veg and non-veg. The incessant ring of mobile phones add to the background din. Losing oneself in a book becomes an impossible feat.

I made my bed on the lower berth. I slept fitfully, having tucked my watch under the pillow. When I woke up after a couple of hours, I instinctively groped under the pillow. The watch was gone.

I searched everywhere – under the berth, inside the sheets, even in bizarre places like the upper berth, where it could only have landed by defying gravity. Desperation crept in.

Fleetingly, I suspected my co-passengers. Could it have been the couple who disembarked at 3 a.m. in Coimbatore? They didn't look like thieves. Could it be the man snoring in the next berth? Surely not – he was sleeping far too soundly. Then where on Earth was my precious watch?

In my mind, I was already filing a police report, making an insurance claim, preparing to argue with the insurance company. I could hear my brother-in-law in Thalassery chiding me:

"Only you would do such a thing!"

"Why carry valuables on a train?"

"You should have taken a flight!"

The loss of something I'd cherished for over four decades hurt. I sat staring through the tinted window, feeling oddly exposed. Over the years, I'd come to believe that while I had it on my wrist, the tutelary spirit of my father protected me. Without it, I felt naked, vulnerable. At least it was insured, I thought. I could use the money to finance my long-planned trip to South America.

As the train neared my destination, I decided to check one last time. Shining my phone's torch under the berth, I spotted a glint in the corner where the side and division bulkheads met the floor. Crawling under, I discovered the tip of the bracelet – the watch was lodged between layers of linoleum. It was as if someone had placed it there deliberately. Perhaps a caprice of my writing fairy? Just so I could write this story!

I was flooded with immense relief – and mild disappointment. The South American adventure would have to wait. I realised then that the watch was more than a sentimental keepsake. It made me feel superhuman.

And no, it's not for sale.

~

4

Room 235

What is special about this card key that occupies a prominent place in my museum of memories? The story may amuse you, but to me it is just one episode from a long list reinforcing my suspicion that I am the unsuspecting protagonist in a never-ending series of the American TV show, *Candid Camera*.

I was in South Tyneside College to attend a course on high voltage electric propulsion, in connection with an investigation. I had rung ahead to a nice hotel located by the sea and asked for a room with a sea view, but when I checked in, I was told that all the rooms with sea views were taken. Nothing new there; I rarely got a hotel room with a view.

Hurrying up to my room, I swiped the key against the door. It would not open. Frustrated, I looked around helplessly. I was late for class. A young hotel maid saw me struggle and came over.

"Let me help you, sir," she offered, and I meekly handed her the key. It didn't work for her either.

"Hmmm. It may be damaged," she said. "So finicky, these plastic keys. I'll get you a new one. Sorry about this, sir."

I did not tell her that it was the story of my life and gave her a doleful look instead. Within minutes, she returned with a new key, and voilà, the door opened.

It was a room with a sea view! Not only that, it was spacious with plush leather furniture and a polished oak floor;

a large bed with goose-down pillows; and glorious white cotton sheets. The fragrance of the orchids on the pillows wafted across the room. Even the maid was surprised at the look of disbelief on my face. I had expected the usual: a dingy room overlooking a moss-laden concrete terrace; polyester fibre pillows that guaranteed insomnia; and mangy, smelly carpets.

'My fortunes have changed, I have escaped from the clutches of the candid camera man,' I thought as I thanked the maid, dumped my suitcase and ran to the class.

It was a good day of learning and I thoroughly immersed myself in the class, forgetting all about the lucky start to my day and the room with a view. After class, I decided to walk back to the hotel. The salty smell of the sea, the throaty lament of the seagulls, and the golden afterglow of twilight – all transported me back to my youth when I sailed the oceans as a marine engineer. Lost in reverie, I reached my hotel in a state of calm and well-being. After a quick shower, a cold beer and dinner, I was ready for bed.

I sank into the soft pillows and scented gossamer sheets. Gently, I transitioned to a make-believe world between wakefulness and sleep, where I always got the things I wanted, where rooms and restaurant tables with views were written into my life's contract, and where my journey on Earth was not signposted by one mishap after another. I yielded to sleep as my rumination on this lucky day mingled with my dreams.

Then I woke up. A big burly man was singing sea shanties in a booming voice as he staggered around the room switching on all the lights. He stood by my bed, swinging a little suitcase and balancing himself as if he was on the deck of a ship at sea. He sang, 'Hey-ho the lazy sailor.' I saw that the giant was ready to collapse on top of me and screamed. The man froze, stopped singing and let out a deep growl like a tiger disturbed while mating. Then, realising his mistake, he turned and headed unsteadily back towards the door.

"Sorry mate, wrong room, wrong room," he mumbled in confusion.

"No worries, just switch off the lights," I was magnanimous.

I slipped back into my orchid-scented dream and woke up in the morning feeling fresh and rested. I was positive the episode of the drunken sailor had taken place in an unreal world.

The next day, the woman who greeted me at the breakfast hall asked for my room number.

"235," I spoke over her head, eyeing several empty tables overlooking the sea. It was getting late for my class and I wanted her to get on with it.

"Mr Warburton? Edward Warburton?" she queried, with a slightly incredulous look.

"No, Chandroth, Gopinath Chandroth."

"No problem, sir. I think they made a mistake on the list. It has Mr Warburton in 235 and yourself in 234. Not to worry, love!" she was apologetic.

As I was half way through breakfast, I had an epiphany: I was allocated room 234, but had occupied 235. That explained why my key hadn't worked. Edward Warburton, the inebriated singer of sea shanties, was not the intruder. I was.

To this day, I wonder where Mr Warburton spent that night!

~

5

A Staircase for Sale

The house of my childhood has been demolished. The staircase, complete, is for sale. It is made of solid wood, of excellent quality. Someone said that one of us should buy it. Buy a staircase? The million times I ran up and down those stairs, chased by my sisters and brothers, running up to complain to father, running down for dinner. If I buy that staircase, with its brass fixtures and its knurled wood banisters, will I hear father coming down in his wooden clogs? See the emerald-green of his eyes? Will my mother give me refuge from the persecuting siblings? I hear the gentle shuffle of her feet.

I see the deer-heads and their disproportionately beautiful antlers. The *punkha*[1] and its pulley. The day I challenged God to place a bicycle in the punkha room by the next morning, as a condition for continuing to believe in Him. That very room where I permanently lost my faith when bleary-eyed and sleepless, I ran in the next morning and saw no shiny new bicycle. The car shed with its deadly repair pit where I challenged the ghosts of Thiyerankunnu to either get me or leave me forever in peace. The *poomukham*[2], where I learned Malayalam and maths from a tuition master. "Draw a loaf of bread," he would say, "now cut it diagonally in half." I learned how to write Ma of Malayalam while learning about diagonals and the abstraction of three-dimensional objects into their projections.

---

1 *Punkha, a traditional hand operated fan operated with a pulley system*

2 *Poomukham, a traditional Kerala style veranda*

Where has the ghost of Madu gone? Still whimpering in the dark *kalavara*[3], now devoid of walls? I smell the mysterious under-stairs *pathayam*[4] with its grains and coconuts. Where, oh where, will those poor Gods go? Mahavishnu and his serpent bed; Siva in his resplendent leopard skin flaunting the menacing trident; Saraswati and her lute; Mahalakshmi and her lotus. Gods and ghosts, wander lost and untethered. No walls to hang from, no people to spook. I must house them before I am done with this story.

I can see the beads of perspiration on my dear aunt's forehead as she toiled with the smoking wood fire in the kitchen. I remember with fondness the young boy employed to look after me. He was only a few years older, but his wild stories enthralled us while the monsoon rains serenaded a magical lullaby outside. Fast forward some years to the machete wound one of us inflicted on his arm while he ground for dosa on the well-worn mortar and pestle. Granite stone turned to marble with decades of grinding. The beads of blood seeped out from the muscle just near his elbow. They looked like little dew drops on the grass. His eyes screamed murder, but he exercised serious self-restraint for a hundred different reasons. One of them being the hopeless poverty he would return to, had he retaliated.

Cricket, played with balls woven from coconut tree leaves and bats shaped from the base of the palm frond. Wickets of sticks, on laterite stone, blood-coloured red dust mixing in with grazed knees and elbows. It was almost every evening after school and before dusk, before the sun set and the sisters

---

3 *Kalavara, a store room.*

4 *Pathayam, a storage area built into the wall or floor for storing grains and other non-perishable food.*

emerged with oil lamps invoking the Gods.

Having lost faith, I smirked silently and wished the dusk wouldn't interrupt the day, which had potential for endless cricket. We had invented a new score, or rather adapted an existing one. It was a century if we could hit the ball over the gate and onto Thiyarankunnu, across the road. A full hundred, if one had the strength to hit that shot.

Was it not on such a cricketing evening that I saw my first white man? Botha van Ingen, coffee planter client, stepped out of his Austin, door held open by his driver. Emerging polished brown shoes, khaki trousers, white shirt, smoking pipe, khaki hat with a brown silk rim. We were frozen like still shots from an old documentary film. Father emerging from his office on to the portico and down to the car porch to meet his old friend and client. Botha's face, I had registered, was blood red. I hadn't seen a face like that ever. Redder than the hibiscus in our garden – and boy the hibiscus was some red. As he passed me, he patted my head. The spell broke. Cricket continued.

I blush to remember the curious incident when I was caught fondling another under the piled law books. Indeed, what about the law books and what about the law? What about those countless clients and peons and poor relatives who used to haunt the office space and its veranda? Or the discreet domestic messages that I took from mother to father as he lectured his clients on points of jurisprudence? The wooden floor upstairs resonating with the patter of children's feet. Father's political speeches echoing across town ricocheted in our ears as we prepared to sleep.

Deep and mysterious well, swallower of cricket balls,

provider of sweet water, I see you still standing. You remember with me, the red tropical frog in the bathroom camouflaged as Lifebuoy soap. Smoke from the water-heating stove diffusing and scattering the weak light from a shade-less low-wattage bulb. I grab the frog, mistaking it for soap, and it quickly jumps out of my hands, scratching my palms with little claws. I give you my story for safekeeping, for I know you will stand forever.

What to do? There is no fuss, there is no resentment. Only a hollow feeling that somehow the ghosts of my past are out in the streets. Where shall I confine them?

How will I fill the void?

The problem has suggested the solution. I have now built a house in my mind and I have connected it to the well that still stands. All the little memories, the big fears, ghosts, spirits, and bicycle-denying Gods now live there, happy and comfortable, in an ever-after sort of permanence. And, no. I don't need that staircase. This mind house has only one storey.

~

6

One Way Ticket for Goats

In the Gorkha district, halfway along the road from Kathmandu to Pokhara, is a temple called Manakamana. It was one of the scheduled stops in our itinerary, and all I knew was that the cable car ride presented spectacular views. No one told me about goats. I was, therefore, perplexed by the fares table: Normal; Student; Elder; Disabled; Child; Indian citizen; Indian child; SAARC; Chinese (adult and child); Foreigner; and 'Goat'. A return fare for a goat was 240 Nepalese rupees.

We boarded a cable car. The car ahead was an open cage for animals. The views were, as promised, heavenly. The Himalayan mountain range in its primeval glory cradled the Trisuli river, the fast-flowing water shimmering in the sun. The verdant splendour of the flora changed rapidly as the car ascended. The icy peaks looked as if sculpted in crystal, and little hutments dotted the near-vertical slopes.

As we stepped off the cable car, we joined the throng of devotees walking to the temple. This is when I noticed goats and roosters among us. The roosters were being carried in large netted bags and the goats were on short lengths of rope. They appeared reluctant to accompany their owners as if they had premonitions of their near future.

We reached the temple, and I quickly figured out why the goats were not too eager to get there. The picture was clear. The faithful went in from one end of the temple, slaughtered the goat, and prayed to the goddess to fulfil their wishes. The carcass blessed by the priest was transformed into *prasad*[5], an offering blessed and sanctified by the goddess. Manakamana, meaning the heart's innermost wishes, was believed by the pious to be granted by a bloodthirsty goddess.

Devotees, their foreheads and hair plastered with blood-red vermilion powder, emerged from the temple carrying the butchered remains of their animals. I saw a couple with a large carrier bag, four black hooves sticking out of it. The smell of blood melded with that of incense, jasmine, and marigold.

The background noise of the crowd's chatter blended with the loud rhythms of drums and traditional wind instruments. The desperate bleating of goats awaiting their impending death reached a crescendo as each animal, I presume, met its end. Not having the heart to witness the sacrifice, I remained outside.

There was a shop outside the temple offering to barbecue the meat. Some surrendered their goat remains to this shop, while others carried them home, a bloody trail in their wake. People trampled on the blood as it mixed with the dust and clotted on the soles of their footwear. New arrivals raced to take their position in the long queue, waiting impatiently for their turn to fulfil their wishes. The poor goats, never eager to keep up with their owners, bleated.

I came away, a deep sadness clouding my view of the Himalayan scenery on my return journey. All I could see was the recalcitrant goat trying to hold back on its four hooves while the faithful dragged it along. Above the whirr of the cable car, I heard its trembling bleat. I hear it now.

---

5 *Prasad, sometimes also called prasadam is an offering of food made to God.*

In my mind, I play a game. Will the goddess grant the wishes of the goat? What would it wish for? What would I wish for? Will my wish or the wish of the hapless creatures ever be fulfilled?

Dear goat, I seek your forgiveness for the wicked foolishness of my species, for the cruel partisan goddess who favours human beings over animals. I bid you farewell and caress your gentle forehead while you wait for your end. Why they charge you for a return ride, I cannot fathom. Is it a cruel joke or a clerical error?

~

7

Language Problem

(A shortened version, 'At sea with words', was published by Deccan Herald, 16 April 2025)

Some years ago, I was in Llandudno, North Wales, on an accident investigation. A ship had been washed ashore and had broken up in the storm. All twenty crew members were picked out of the icy water and airlifted to safety by the coastguard. They were Polish nationals and spoke very little English.

We hired a meeting room in a local hotel. Interviewing the traumatised crew, one by one, with the help of an interpreter, was exhausting. After five interviews, I decided to get some fresh air. Walking around in the garden outside, I saw one of the crew members smoking a cigarette under a tree. He was the large able-bodied seaman (AB) with a walrus moustache, the second witness I had interviewed that morning. I was aware the ship owner was arranging a bus to repatriate them to Poland. Walking over, I made conversation,

"You go home tomorrow?"

"You what?" he looked puzzled. Language problem, I figured.

Poking him in the chest with my index finger, I spoke slowly and clearly.

"You," I said, pointing east (in the general direction of Poland), "go – home – HOME. Go home bus."

I mimicked a bus driver driving a bus with its low-set steering wheel. Getting carried away with my charade and remembering an Indian state transport bus of the 70s, I squeezed an imaginary rubber horn with my right hand while continuing to steer deftly with my left.

"Pom Pom."

He looked at me in bewilderment. It was as if he didn't trust his eyes and his ears. PTSD, my well-honed sense of empathy advised me. I too would feel the same if my ship had broken up into pieces. I didn't give up and, for further clarity, used the double-shift gear stick to move up a gear or two. No comprehension, not yet.

Just then, a woman joined us. The AB turned to her and said, "See if you can help him, Lucy. He doesn't speak much English, and I haven't the foggiest idea what he's trying to tell me."

And just as I was beginning to understand the situation, the real AB with the walrus moustache walked past us, shouting at someone on his phone in Polish.

~

8

Horrible Homophones

(A shortened version, 'The son, the sun and the slip-up', was published by the Deccan Herald, 4 January 2025)

"English is a funny language. They write 'CAT,' pronounce it 'KAT,' and it means 'Poocha,' We write 'Poocha,' pronounce it 'Poocha,' and it means 'Poocha,'" a man from Kerala once said.

I tend to agree with this man. It is indeed a funny language. Otherwise, why pronounce two words exactly the same when they are spelled differently? Take the example of SUN and SON, for instance. Or HEIR and AIR. Or BEAR and BARE. They hide behind the respectability of the posh-sounding word *homophone*. But they serve no purpose other than to cause confusion and get me into trouble. I would ask the experts to review these troublesome words and weed out the duplicates.

One day, I took my wife to this lakeside café in a place called West Wellow in Hampshire. The best toasties in England are to be had there – tomatoes, onions, and cheese between two slices of generously buttered white bread, toasted to golden perfection, consumed with a bit of salad and washed down with a pot of tea. Delightful, more so after a gruelling bike ride in sub-zero temperatures. I had been here three or four times but with a cycling group.

The sun had emerged after several days of hiding behind the clouds. My wife is not a cyclist, so we drove there. It is owned by a friendly, middle-aged couple. The husband greeted us as we entered. I assumed he had recognised me, having forgotten to factor in a small detail – he had only seen me in my cycling paraphernalia: all bright orange and yellow high-vis Lycra, wraparound sunglasses, and a helmet. That morning, I was in my civvies. As far as he was concerned, he was seeing me for the first time in his life.

So, when he said, "You brought the sun with you today," I thought he meant, *instead of bringing your cycling friends, you brought your son today.* I was a bit taken aback and turned around to take a good look at my wife, as if I were seeing her for the first time. I tried to understand why the man mistook her for my son.

Then I had it figured out – it was the short haircut that gave her a boyish look.

"No," I replied. "This is my wife." The moment I said it, I realised my error.

The restaurateur mumbled something, and I wished I were a slice of tomato hidden inside a toastie.

Anyway, the moment had passed, and no explanation was offered. The toastie was delicious, as always, maybe flavoured with a touch of foolishness.

All because of a damned homophone!

~

9

Duality

This story attempts to illustrate how our dormant identities shape our worldview, and how transient these identities truly are. The corollary is that although our worldviews may differ, essentially it is the same world we argue about. It is only human fallibility that makes us view the world from a single perspective and deny all others. Man's worst enemy is his dogma.

Many years ago I was visiting my sister who lived in Malakkallu (Kerala), at the southern end of the 1,000-mile-long mountain range that bisects the Indian Peninsula. I had acquired a new camera and intended to capture the sights of Kerala for my friends back in London.

When I looked around, however, I saw only mundane, everyday sights: cashew fruits in bright yellows and reds, translucent orange mangoes falling in the wind, oversized and abundant jackfruit with their succulent flesh hidden by the spiked outer skin, hibiscus flowers spilling over the fences, and the occasional goat lazily nibbling at them, coconut and betel nut trees competing to canopy the clear blue skies, precarious bamboo bridges swaying in the wind, the shy touch-me-not leaves closing in on themselves on contact, and a myriad other sights. Nothing novel to photograph.

It was my sister's 60th birthday. A priest conducted ancient Vedic rites in her honour, chanting Sanskrit verses and gesticulating with timeless gestures. The ritual fire, fed with the occasional spoon of ghee, leaped and raged. A mother hen chaperoned her chicks, feeding them grains scattered across the hard, earthen courtyard. The mountain stream flowed nearby, and a cement tank interspersed in its path sparkled with clear fresh water, forever overflowing back into the stream. The delighted cries of little children splashing about mingled with the mantras invoked by the priest.

I sat there mesmerised by the flames of the sacred fire, the air intense with the smell of burning ghee and camphor. There I was: born here, grew up here, part of the scene in every sense. I slipped into a semi-trance, induced by the evocative smells and sounds. I had moved beyond the present as I floated on the magic carpet of happy childhood memories. The spirits of my departed parents smiled upon me.

Suddenly and without warning, I thought of London. I was trudging across London Bridge on my daily march to work. I thought of my home in England: the breathtaking beauty of magnolias in April, the daffodils and cherry blossoms of spring, the robins, the swallows, and the blackbird. I was suddenly homesick! I missed my family and friends back in London. I longed for the Guardian newspaper there and then.

I was sitting in one part of the world and missing another. I was curiously happy and thankful for this dichotomy. The existential concepts of the West – free will, choice, and personal responsibility – sat comfortably with my Eastern Karma and its very diminution of the self. *Sarvam Maya* – 'All you behold is an illusion' – seemed more palatable in that fleeting moment. I observed the dualities of my mind with an objectivity that comes to one at rare moments. I felt thankful for everything: for my past and my present, for my mental reconciliation of divergent philosophies, and above all for my feeling of comfort with them.

Almost without thinking, I started seeing the sights I had grown up with as if for the first time. I photographed everything – the jackfruit, the cashew, the untranslatable vegetables, and the misty mountains. Even the stark, unforgiving laterite soil where I had grazed my knees as a child.

I was a complete man of dual identities – both transient, both illusory.

~

10

The Weight of Smoke

(A version of this story was published by The Times of India, 26 May 2025)

Studying the colour of smoke from the chimney of the Sistine Chapel has an interesting marine parallel. For a very different reason, marine engineers too are very keen to observe the colour of smoke from the funnel of their ship. It is their chimney, and the engine room of the ship, their chapel.

The engine room is a complex and compact space packed to the brim with a vast array of machinery systems. A ship is a floating hotel but with exceptions: it has no access to shore-based services. Giant propulsion engines as tall as double-storeyed buildings; power plants and boilers sufficient to meet the needs of a small township; air-conditioning systems; sewage treatment units; and desalination plants – the ship has it all.

The marine engineer is the jack and master of all machinery. They need to have an intimate understanding, not only of the functioning of the equipment, but also the thermodynamics of the processes within, the hydraulic flows and the mechanical stresses involved. They need to know like the back of their hands, the labyrinthine pipework and electrical circuits that service the equipment. It is no easy task being a marine engineer. A single mistake can lead to multiple and often catastrophic failures.

The last thing a marine engineer wants is a breakdown of critical items of machinery in the middle of the ocean thousands of miles from help. I too was a serving marine engineer on large merchant ships. As chief engineer, one loses the gut instinct developed by spending most of the working day in proximity to machinery. The chief is normally buried in paperwork. This is why they watch smoke, which has an uncanny knack of revealing the state of health of the engines and boilers.

Every evening, after dinner, I walked the length of the main deck, frequently looking up at the funnel to study the colour of smoke. Black means poor combustion indicating problems with the engine. White – water ingress into the combustion space, and blue implies excessive consumption of lubricating oil. Sparks from the funnel? Time to don the boiler suit. Near-colourless smoke was the Holy Grail, something rarely seen but aspired to, nevertheless.

On one occasion, I observed thick black smoke and hoped we could deal with the problem in port. Sadly, it culminated in the immobilisation of our ship for nearly 24 hours, while we replaced a piston weighing over a tonne in the middle of a raging Atlantic storm. Our fully loaded 50,000-tonne vessel was flung about like a piece of flotsam. We could barely stand without holding on to something. I'll never forget how helpless we felt that night.

And so, just as the colour of smoke is interpreted by the faithful gathered in St. Peter's Square as a sign to humanity, the colour of smoke at the funnel is a portent for what lies ahead for the marine engineer. Whether generated from the holy precincts of the Sistine Chapel, or from the internal combustion engines of a ship, the smoke is not just exhaust, but something weighed in hope, peace of mind and certitude.

~

11

Pretty Preity's Dainty Dimples

Despite being reasonably skilled at warding off scammers, I have less success with clever salespeople. They often talk me into purchasing things and services I don't need.

Take Sky, for example: I used to have the basic service and was quite content with it. The only sport I really like is cricket. For this, a one-month contract is ideal. You could order the service and give your notice of cancellation the next day, if you plan it well. I just watch the big events like the World Cup or test match series where India would be playing. In spite of having spent half my life in England, and the affection I have for my adopted country, my loyalty when it comes to cricket, lies wholly and squarely with the Indian cricket team. Sorry Norman Tebbit – your loyalty test is based on a false premise.

Anyway, a year ago, I had taken up a one month subscription to the Cricket channel on Sky Sports. I called them the next day to give the cancellation notice. But here is where my plan fell apart. The sales guy, based in India, knew a thing or two about my psychology that I myself wasn't aware of. To say he was persuasive is like saying Shakespeare could write. He was the master of his art.

The salesman convinced me that I needed the full package: all sports channels from archery to zorbing, the complete movie channel with a monthly free ticket to the cinemas (only Vue cinema), Discovery + and I forget what else. The thing I forgot was that only cricket interested me. I already subscribe to several movie channels and we rarely visit the cinema. I am morally opposed to buying overpriced popcorn. Without eyes one can't see a movie in a cinema. These days it's the same with popcorn.

The salesman had that special talent for saying the right things, he was pressing all the right buttons – You are paying £X already. With just a bit more, a fractional x, added to the extant X, you will have ALL the movie channels, the COMPLETE sports channels, two free tickets to the cinema, every month. The way he intoned 'complete' made me feel that my life was somehow incomplete without the full package. He achieved his target – another sucker succumbed.

I ended up signing a 24-month contract paying nearly 2X because he subsequently loaded on additional channels, like documentaries and music. By then I was putty in his deft hands. He could have sold me the embroidery channel if such a thing existed.

That was a long-winded way of explaining how I ended up watching the Indian Premier League (IPL) cricket finals on 3 June. Why IPL? You might ask. Only because I had access to it although in years past I had felt no inclination for this format of the game. It was a contest between Royal Challengers Bangalore (RCB) and Punjab Super Kings (PBKS), both teams equally strong but RCB with the celebrity Virat Kohli on its side. I decided therefore to support PBKS – I always gun for the underdog.

Another factor that featured in my loyalty calculus was that while RCB is owned by a faceless distillery company, PBKS is co-owned by Preity Zinta, a Bollywood film actress who, although past her heyday, sports two endearing dimples on her cheeks. They really come into their own when she smiles. I wanted to see her happy. That required PBKS to win.

Sadly, although they came within touching distance of winning the game, PBKS lost by six runs. Zinta's dimples retreated behind a nimbus cloud that darkened her face.

No cup for PBKS, no display of delectable dimples for me. Immediately after the match, I called Sky to cancel the Sports and Movies package. They sold me their broadband service instead.

~

12

The Elusive Reflection

Kottuvayalil Subramanyam Sivasankaran, let's call him Kottu, woke earlier than usual. He didn't expect the day to be any different. His life was eventless, just one continuous tedium of waking up, carrying out his morning routines, walking around his fields and instructing the hired labour to plant this crop and pull out that stump, or cut a channel from the stream to irrigate his banana trees. An early lunch and siesta, a bit of reading and writing until dinner, and then bed before ten. He woke up with the crows. Nothing changed around him except for the seasons – they too seemed to merge into one another – the rain, the sweltering heat, and the rain again.

Kottu lived alone, preferring to keep his own company. He was an enigma to the villagers. Some even called him strange, although no one could deny he had the looks of a film star – sparkling eyes that seemed to look through you, an aquiline nose that contrasted with a strong and straight jaw, a muscular physique and curly black hair.

Women openly lusted after him, but he paid them no attention. His behaviour was not that of a 25-year-old man with rampant hormones. He was the opposite, exuding an air of saintly detachment. Persistent rumours suggested he was impotent. The more educated among them maintained that Kottu was asexual, one of the lucky 1% of the human race.

That morning, as always, Kottu glanced at himself in the

full-length mirror by his bed. He paused. It was disorienting, as if he'd missed a step on a familiar staircase. His reflection was missing – not even a faint shadow. Everything else in the room was there: the bed, stacks of dusty books on the shelves, the furniture. He could even see the objects directly behind him, as if he were transparent – and he actually was. The mirror gave no sign of his presence, as though he'd been airbrushed out of a digital image.

A faint chill crept through the room, and for a moment the air felt heavier, charged with something unspoken. Kottu ran to another mirror, then tried every mirror in the house. It was the same. He was missing from every reflection. Slapping himself and tugging at his earlobes, he confirmed he wasn't dreaming. His placid lifestyle was suddenly upended by this bizarre turn of events. Disconcerted, he decided to go for a walk, hoping the fresh air would clear his mind.

Crossing the paddy field, he noticed the birds were silent, and the usual morning sounds seemed muffled. The first person he saw was the neighbouring farmer, Velayudhan Sadasivan Bhattathiripad, Velu for short. Velu was still some distance away, but Kottu could clearly hear his words. Curiously, Velu hadn't opened his mouth until then. So, what was he hearing? Kottu walked up to him and said,

"I'm sorry, Velu, I just don't have the money to lend you."

Velu's mouth gaped open as if some spring holding his jaws together had released. He had never asked Kottu for money. He was desperate that day and was on his way to Kottu's house to touch him for a small loan. But he was only rehearsing the request in his mind. He hadn't said a word.

Then how did Kottu know? The situation was so weird that

Velu didn't think of denying that he was looking for a loan.

Both of them stared at each other in total disbelief. Velu was wondering how Kottu read his mind and Kottu was equally incredulous. Strange things were happening to him. He continued to hear Velu think as if he were speaking aloud – How did Kottu know? Does he know about my financial difficulties in the new grocery business? That I am being threatened by the moneylender? His mind raced away.

Kottu placed a hand on his shoulder.

"I don't know about your difficulties, Velu. No. Nothing about the moneylender, either. I didn't know you needed money until I saw you this morning."

Velu hastily walked away, his face contorted in sheer horror and confusion. Kottu stood panting, almost struggling to breathe. Could this be happening? First the missing reflection, then the mind-reading business. He decided to continue his walk, his mind completely unable to grapple with the torrent of inexplicable events of the day.

A young woman was walking towards him. He recognised her – Koodali Thazhathuveettil Shyamaladevi, Shama, who worked at the only bank in the village. In her early twenties, she was a diffident and demure woman, rarely making eye contact with anyone. She was popularly known as Shy Shama. Kottu did not greet her but they briefly exchanged smiles, the customary mode of greeting in Kerala.

As they passed each other, Kottu heard her thoughts. It was straight out of some smutty erotic literature he had come across as a schoolboy. He could not bear to repeat her thoughts to himself – they were beyond crude, but worst of all, involved him. Not knowing how to react, he kept a straight face.

Something strange was stirring in his groin area, although he had never experienced the phenomenon.

Kottu continued on his walk. He didn't talk to anyone or react to anyone's thoughts. Some were kind, but many were rife with nastiness and jealousy. The most common were – 'here comes the weirdo' and 'what a waste of a man!'

Unable to bear the innuendos, the snide remarks, the sheer ill-will of the villagers, he returned home.

The rest of the day was uneventful. His mind was a roiling ocean, unable to make sense of what was happening. His reflection was still missing. He went to sleep early that evening just to get some respite from the dominating thought – that he was teetering on the verge of madness.

The next morning, Kottu woke up with the sun. Strangely, the thought of Shama was foremost in his mind. He ran to the mirror. There he was, in full and original form, his reflection back to normal except for one change – a giant erection protruding like a monument to his lost stoicism, and hopefully, the telepathy.

~

13

Upper Class Travel

There is a popular story in India about Sudha Murthy, the wife of the software billionaire Narayan Murthy and mother-in-law of former British Prime Minister Rishi Sunak.

The Murthys have retained their humility despite their immense wealth – which has only increased their popularity among the Indian public. Once, Sudha was standing in line at the business class check-in for some international flight out of an Indian airport. As always, she was dressed in a plain, unassuming cotton saree. The person behind her is said to have told her,

"Ma'am, economy is over there!"

So much for making assumptions and the signs of unconscious bias. But these things happen to everyone. It happened to me as well. My only excuse is that I was still a young lad of 19 at the time.

I had gone to spend my Dussehra holidays with my sister in Kasaragod. Just like the students of today, the students of the '70s were also skint. We travelled third class and didn't make a reservation just to save a few rupees. The journey – lasting two nights and three days from Calcutta to Kasaragod in an unreserved third-class compartment on an Indian train of the '70s – was something else. If you were lucky, you could occupy the luggage rack and get some sleep. If not, you perched with half a bum at the edge of a seat originally designed for three but usually occupied by six. If you got up, you lost your seat. If you left your patch of space on the luggage berth to use the toilet, someone else occupied it. The railways went to great lengths to ensure the facilities were functional and devoid of any vestige of comfort. The seats were hardwood with no upholstery.

So, imagine my delight when my brother-in-law surprised me by gifting me a first class ticket for the return journey to Calcutta. As I was boarding the empty compartment, which proudly displayed my name among a printed list of privileged first class passengers, he advised me,

"Don't let all and sundry get into the first class."

First class and third class were like heaven and hell. As the inferior classes filled up, some people tried to barge into the first class. My brother-in-law probably had this in mind when he advised me. But discretion is not an attribute associated with 19-year-olds. I took his counsel to heart and decided to implement it without fear or favour.

I was the only occupant in a coach that comprised some five or six spacious cabins with their own individual doors and plush cushioned interiors. Most cabins had four berths, while some were coupés with two berths – preferred by honeymooners and other amorous couples.

The train arrived at Payyannur, approximately an hour later. I was walking the corridor, determined to deny entry to anyone who tried. I noticed someone trying to open the rear door and promptly locked it from the inside using the heavy steel latches provided. A young gentleman with a very severe moustache looked quite puzzled and upset when he saw what I had done. He was accompanied by a whole bunch of soldiers in military green uniform – boots and all. Then he said, with some urgency in his voice,

"Please open the door."

The train was scheduled to stop there only for a short time. I simply shook my head. The conversation was monosyllabic.

"No!"

"No?" The soldiers joined their leader in a chorus of incredulity.

"No." I was firm.

There was no time to argue. The gentleman and his platoon ran to the other end of the coach. They ran fast and in step. The sound of their boots on the concrete platform, loud and rhythmic, evoked visions of galloping wild stallions. I outran them – from the inside – and locked the front door as well.

"Open the bloody door," the distressed passenger was red with all the running and uncontrolled fury. I couldn't understand why he wouldn't go to his own second or third class compartment. Nevertheless, I owed him an explanation, I thought. So I said,

"Ayyoo, this is first class!"

He replied,

"Do you think only you can travel by first class? Open the damn door, NOW!"

The train was hooting, ready to depart. I let him in. He was a serving captain travelling on a warrant issued by the Indian army. He had more rights to first class travel than I did. He was travelling to Calcutta as well. We exchanged addresses before we parted.

Only last week, my sister was travelling from London to Bangalore via Frankfurt. Her flight was late getting into Frankfurt, and she was worried she was going to miss the connecting flight. She arrived at the departure gate and pushed through a large throng of people waiting at the counter.

"Excuse me, excuse me," she said as she inched her way frantically to the front of the crowd. Then someone in a wrinkled old kurta told her,

"We're all waiting for the same flight."

"But I am in business class," my sister insisted.

"We're all business class," said the kurta man! It transpired he was travelling with his wife – a famous Bollywood singer.

So, the moral of the story is... I don't know what it is – but I just love telling these funny stories!

~

14

What's in a Name?

(A shortened version, 'Becoming Namewise', was published by Deccan Herald, 24 August 2024)

My mother once asked me to get some vegetables from the market. It was a long time ago, and we had just moved to Delhi from the south. Hindi, the local language, was an alien language for me. I went to the market and was shocked beyond belief: the entire place reverberated with the sound of my name – Gobi Gobi Gobi. Why were so many strangers calling out to me? I am famous, my 14-year-old mind reasoned irrationally.

In a short while, I made an observation that both explained the mystery and deflated my ego. Each vegetable vendor was holding out a cauliflower or a cabbage, intent on demonstrating how much bigger and fresher their vegetables were. Gobi, it turned out, is the generic name in Hindi for the family of cruciferous vegetables. Phool Gobi (Flower Gobi) is cauliflower, and Bandh Gobi (Closed Gobi) is cabbage.

Often people misspell my name. People often address me as Gobi in emails. I take such opportunities to correct them – in jest, of course. 'My name is spelt Gopi, not Gobi,' I would write to them. 'Gobi means cauliflower or cabbage in Hindi.' Most people see the funny side of it but immediately stop misspelling my name.

Another concern is people not using my name at all. It has a similar effect on me as when people don't make eye contact or, worse, look at someone else while answering my question. I attend Pilates lessons at our local gym three days a week. The class is always full, and Janet, the instructor, addresses everyone by name. Everyone, that is, who has a traditional British name.

"Tuck your chin, Daniel," or "Margaret, don't hold your breath," or "Very good, Emily," she would say. However, she never used my name. The gym app for booking classes clearly shows who is attending which class. Under my photograph, my name, Gopi, is written. I hadn't included my surname, just to make it a bit easier for others. It should have been easy enough to remember my name. Why didn't she use it then? I couldn't understand it. Janet is a sweet and affable woman. She is not a bigot, by any stretch of the imagination. Then why – why? Like sand in my shoes, it was grating. One day, after nearly a year had passed, I approached her once the Pilates students had left the room. Janet was packing up.

"Janet, do you know my name?" I asked with a smile. I didn't want to come across as being upset.

"Yes," she replied with a slight touch of hesitation, "Go... Go... Gopi?" Then, the poor woman clarified, as if reading my mind. "I was afraid of mispronouncing and causing offence."

After that day, she used my name liberally, as if she had named me in her arms as a newborn. As they say, you can't make an omelette without breaking an egg.

I remember my college mate, Subramanian, being called Submaranian by a lecturer at the South Shields marine college. The lecturer was being playful and said it with a smile. That was the tongue-in-cheek, non-PC humour of the '80s. Funny, nevertheless.

Talking about recent times, my friend and neighbour Paul could not, for the life of him, remember my wife Sujata's name. He knew it started with an S and ended with an A. He picked a random name each time he addressed her: Sangita, Sunita, Sarita, Sulekha, Sucheta... Anything but Sujata.

One Christmas, following the local custom, we dropped greeting cards through our neighbours' letterboxes. My Christmas card to Paul read, 'Merry Christmas. From Gopi, Sujata, Savita, Surekha, Sangita, Sunita, and the rest of the harem.'

I saw Paul a few days after Christmas. "You know Monty," he said, smiling with a paternal hand on my shoulder, "after I saw your card, I wrote her name on a piece of paper and stuck it on the fridge. S U J A T A – I'll never forget it now."

Monty was the name of our chocolate Labrador.

~

15

Speaking Like a Native

Yesterday, I was asked to teach English to a student from the Middle East. He has good spoken English skills and so I asked him,

"What is your ultimate goal with the English lessons?"

"To be able to speak like a native speaker," he responded.

My first reaction was panic. That's because I'm a very literal person. I take most things literally and often miss the figurative meaning of things. I nearly told him that I could certainly teach him to speak like a native, but with an Indian accent.

This is not a new problem. As a 14-year-old, I opted for Higher Hindi in school. We had moved to Delhi from Kerala and the only Hindi I knew was to ask someone's name and their age (तुम्हारा नाम क्या है? तुम्हारी उम्र क्या है?) The other option was to take Higher Sanskrit. But Sanskrit was taught in Hindi and my young mind decided that I would be dealing with double the trouble by opting for Sanskrit.

How wrong I was! It was extremely hard to achieve a good score in Hindi. Even the locals struggled to get above 50%. Sanskrit, on the other hand, was a doddle. The lowest mark anyone got was 60%. Anyway, my Hindi learning curve was so steep that I often stumbled.

What got to me was the concept of metaphors and the sayings that make use of them. And there were several. One of them, ऊँट के मुँह में जीरा ('oont ke mooh mem jeera') or a cumin seed in the mouth of a camel, confounded me. Once we were told to make a sentence that illustrates the meaning of this saying. So, I made up this elaborate story about a Bedouin Arab and his camel sweltering in the desert heat for days on end. Finally, they reached an oasis, whereupon he fed the camel a single cumin seed. The camel then remarked with disdain, "A cumin seed in the mouth of a camel?"

I received a zero.

There were other sayings like Gangaram went to Ganga and Jamunadas went to Jamuna, which basically means (I figured this out after I had failed Hindi) everyone went his own way. I blush to remember the story I made up about that one, with similar end results.

Zero.

It took me a while to grasp the concept of metaphors. These days, when people ask me to do little consultancy jobs but offer peanuts as remuneration, I ask them, "Are you offering a cumin seed to a camel?" Even non-Hindi speakers instinctively understand me. All I can say is, some crucial part was missed when I was being put together.

Anyway, that's water under the bridge now, so to speak – as you can see, I understand the concept now. But I must've taken my metaphors too seriously. Just the other day, my friend Tom was describing a mutual friend,

"I just love Dan," he says, "he's so sweet. Such a decent chap. Butter wouldn't melt."

The butter bit was new to me. Never having heard the expression before, I researched it and asked a few of my friends, including a grammarian. The conclusion was that Tom was using the expression incorrectly. The expression 'butter wouldn't melt in his mouth' implies that the person comes across as sweet and decent, but deep down, they're a bit of a meanie.

The next time I met Tom over a coffee, I asked him,

"You know, the other day you were talking about Dan and how butter wouldn't melt in his mouth?"

"Yes?"

"Do you know what 'butter wouldn't melt' really means?"

"Oh yeah. It means he's a sweet chap."

"No, it means the opposite. Though I know exactly what you mean, someone else may completely misunderstand you."

Tom was not happy with me and accused me of challenging him. He informed me that he's been speaking English all his life and that expressions should be understood based on the context they're used in, and so on. We had a bit of an argument. I told him that with this particular expression he's been using it the wrong way all his life, that figurative expressions relying on metaphors cannot be context-sensitive because that would make the English language unusable. Tom stopped talking to me.

Indians are quite sensitive about their English language proficiency. You could correct someone's Hindi or Tamil or any of the Indian languages that happen to be their mother tongue. But correct their English and you're in trouble.

"Don't you know English?" is one of the most insulting things you can say to an Indian.

Colonial hangover, what else? But I never imagined an English person could get upset when their English is corrected. I had forgotten there's no colonial effect in England. The Roman conquest was way back in the forgotten past.

Coming back to my student, I'll try to speak with a neutral accent, but apologies in advance if I don't teach you a posh one. You will not speak like an Etonian but like an alumnus of Kendriya Vidyalaya. On the bright side, you'll be able to communicate seamlessly with 1.4 billion Indians with the accent you'll pick up from me.

~

16

The Caves of Cheddar Gorge

Clichés such as 'timeless' and 'time stands still' are often used to describe places: the caves of Cheddar Gorge defy such triteness. Their near ethereal splendour cannot be measured in temporal units. They are today, yesterday and tomorrow. Ignore their physical geology, and you experience the true essence of Time.

The internals of the caves are carved into extraordinary shapes by the seeping water. They look like some postmodern sculpture, every nook and cranny uniquely formed and contoured, imbued with brilliant russet and pink and green. Time has neither stood still nor advanced. It is everywhere, the dripping water of the present, the stalagmites and stalactites of the past and present – a chain of events separated only by microseconds but strung together in millennia, and a future perhaps no different from the past – unpredictable, but with a trajectory well established. Time dilates and contracts simultaneously like some abstruse concept in quantum physics. An illusion of reality manifests in front of you, within your grasp one moment, and slipping out the next.

You leave the caves of Cheddar Gorge with a mind that is frantic in its attempt to find its place in this vast continuum. You wonder if Time itself is that elusive God we argue about, the omnipresent and omnipotent, the eternal, the merciful and the timeless.

~

17

Pico de Gallo

They say half knowledge is dangerous. I say, not if it leads to a story. Last week I was on a business trip to Campo de Gibraltar, a region in the province of Andalusia, Spain. I never miss an opportunity that involves travelling to Spain. I have this misplaced self-concept about being a semi-fluent Spanish speaker! Nothing could be further from the truth. But it is the self-image – what you convince yourself about yourself – that matters. Secretly, I believe I could give Gabriel Garcia Márquez a run for his money, if only I could improve my grammar and vocabulary.

The Mexican restaurant where I had dinner one evening had a menu of 50 dishes. Of these, just two were suitable for vegetarians. A measly looking green leaf against each indicated they were meat-free. Appalling, this discrimination against vegetarians! But on the bright side, I had just two options to choose from, and I went for the burrito.

My order arrived just as I finished my beer. It was tasty, but unlike a South Indian thali, which has a multitude of mini dishes that surprise one's palate with each bite, the burrito tastes the same from beginning to end. Bored with the monotony, I decided to brush up on my Spanish.

The description of the burrito on the menu began: 'Con salteado de verduras y champiñones,' which I mentally translated to 'With salted vegetables and mushrooms.' Wait. That can't be right. Salted vegetables sound so boring. My translation app quickly confirmed my suspicion: 'salteado' means sautéed, not salted. Confidence slightly shaken, I struggled along reading all of the ten items that made up the dish. I recognized some words like guacamole and maiz, while others had to be looked up. Then I stumbled on 'pico de gallo,' which to my horror translates to 'beak of rooster!' I was aghast. The green leaf on the menu was there in error or the Spaniards don't understand the concept of vegetarianism. I felt like a pious Brahmin (a member of a Hindu priestly caste) who was tricked into eating beef.

Summoning the waitress, I protested in pidgin Spanish,

"Me vegetarian. This burrito – it got chicken. No good, señorita."

What next – chicken feathers? I wanted to ask but didn't know the word for feather.

"I am so sorry, sir," she said, her face a deep crimson, "I will change it straight away."

She cast furtive glances at my dinner, scanning for the uninvited chicken. Then she picked up the plate and went into the kitchen at the other end of the restaurant.

A couple of minutes later, she emerged – not with a replacement burrito but with my half-eaten one. Looking neither embarrassed nor apologetic, her face said she had the answer. I guessed the chef was somehow involved in solving the conundrum. Pointing at my burrito, she gently but firmly asked, "Could you please show me the chicken?"

Instead of rooting through the dish, I pointed to 'pico de gallo' in the description, tapping it with my forefinger for emphasis. The smile that lit up her face was that of a mother pardoning an errant child. What she then rattled off was beyond me, but I got the gist – 'pico de gallo' is just the name of a Mexican salad containing tomatoes, jalapeño, and other harmless vegetables. It has nothing to do with the body parts of a rooster.

I finished the rest of the humble pie – sorry, burrito – and left the waitress a generous tip in compensation. The self-confidence in my Spanish has taken a minor beating. Nothing that cannot be fixed with another trip to Spain. The cinema of my life continues.

~

18

Breakfast at Josie's

Our son Siddharth came home one Saturday with his girlfriend Megan. It was Mother's Day on Sunday which was also St. Patrick's Day. On Sunday morning, Sid decided we were all going out for breakfast as a Mother's Day treat. We drove to our local Josie's in Chandler's Ford. The place was heaving, and people were queuing up like young club-goers on a Friday night. We were told there was approximately an hour's wait for a table. The next one was in Romsey, which was also full. Sid then decided we should go to the one in Alresford, a twenty-minute drive away. By the time we arrived, it was nearly noon, and travelling on empty stomachs in the backseat of a car driven by an impatient 24-year-old, both my wife and I were beginning to feel a bit queasy. But at last, we reached our destination, parked up, and walked into Josie's.

"We are not yet officially open," the host told us. "Today is a *soft launch* for friends and family." The phrase soft launch was new to me, but I wanted some food, and the enhancement of my vocabulary did not stop my head from spinning. With envy, I eyed the friends and family tucking into stacks of pancakes with strawberries, eggs benedict, and fresh orange juice. I couldn't bear it, so I moved back towards the road, looking for another place to eat, expecting the rest of the family to follow. But they were still in deep discussion with the host. I went back in just as the host was leading them to a table. Apparently, Sid had told him how he had come down from Bristol to see us, his parents, how today's breakfast was a Mother's Day treat, and how we had driven twenty minutes to get here, and so on. I don't know where he got his tact and powers of persuasion from. Not from me! I take No for an answer much too readily.

To just say the breakfast was delicious would be to undermine the other qualities that make a meal enjoyable. The atmosphere, the service, and the general bonhomie were beyond excellent. We were repeatedly offered more hot drinks and made to feel at home. Just as we were congratulating each other on our lucky day to have gained access to an exclusive event, a lady came to our table and introduced herself.

"Good morning, I'm Josie," she said.

I wasn't sure I had heard her right. A silent question raged through my mind. *You mean you are THE Josie?* The four of us looked at one another and instantly recognised that we were all asking the same silent question. The lady, dressed in green in honour of St. Patrick's Day, certainly didn't act like the boss. She was jovial, friendly, and one with her staff, serving food and chatting to customers.

What she said to us next not only confirmed her proprietorship but also made our day.

"Everything is on the house today. Please ask if you need anything."

Thank you, Josie, for your generosity. You just got yourself four loyal customers.

Thank you, Siddharth, your Mother's Day present was very much appreciated by your mother (and father). Thank you, Sujata, for being the primary reason for our adventure. Thank you, Megan, for the affection you bestow on our son.

And thank you, St. Patrick, for blessing us with so much joy on your special day.

~

19

Music Lessons

(A version, 'From Ship to stage in 90 days...', was published by Deccan Herald, 22 August 2025)

I have never been formally instructed in music. Yet I constantly sing or whistle to myself. My ex-colleagues long suffered this habit as we drove across the United Kingdom investigating marine accidents. I once shared a flat with a friend in Southampton. When I was moving out, he said to me, "I will miss your 5 a.m. singing!" I had always thought I was especially quiet in the mornings so as not to disturb him.

As a young marine engineer, I lived with my parents in Mysore when I came home from the ships. One morning, as I observed the placid and sleepy world pass by from the comfort of an easy chair, someone opened the front gate. A man in the traditional South Indian garb of a spotlessly white *dhoti* and an *angavastram* draped across his bare upper body came through to the veranda. He had the characteristic marks of a scholar – three vertical lines in sandalwood paste on the forehead and an elegant kudumi at the back of his neatly tonsured head. He looked to be in his sixties and exuded an air of authority. Large brown eyes framed by an endearing face commanded instant respect.

"Namaskaram sir, I'm a music teacher," he announced. "If there are children in the house, I can give them lessons."

I told him that I was the youngest of the household. At 26, I could not call myself a child. He was not dissuaded. He could clearly read my mind or at least read the disappointment on my face.

"Adults can learn music too. I could teach you if you like."

Now, I had never considered taking music lessons. My life being split between the sea and land, there was no opportunity to embark on such a learning project either. I replied,

"Unfortunately, I work on ships. I have only three months before I rejoin."

"That's plenty of time. Start tomorrow and you'll be giving a concert before you leave."

He was persuasive and pulled all my strings. I had always suspected there was a musician trapped inside me, and here was my Guru, come to set my talent free.

I didn't need further encouragement. I agreed. He asked me to be ready the next day with a picture of Saraswati, a coconut, and the other paraphernalia for the Guru *puja*. His fee of three thousand rupees was to be paid in advance. He could teach me instrumental or vocals. If I wanted to learn an instrument, I had to buy two violins – one for me and one for him! At ten grand a piece, the violin option was expensive. I chose the cheaper option of singing. The Guru left with a smile, the morning sun eclipsed by the glow on his beaming face.

My mother had only seen him leave and asked me who he was. I informed her that he was to be my music teacher and we were embarking on a project to turn me into a professional Carnatic music vocalist in three months. Could she please get everything ready for the Guru puja while I pop to the bank to withdraw his fee?

"Are you mad?" she asked, her hand on her partly open mouth in the typical Indian gesture of incredulity.

She couldn't believe my naïveté and quickly convinced me that I was being had. As a young woman, she had been formally instructed in South Indian classical music for over a decade. I couldn't argue with her.

"I'll talk to him tomorrow," she reassured me.

The teacher arrived early the next morning. The conversation between him and my mother went something like this:

"Sir, did you tell my son he would be giving a vocal performance in three months?"

"Hmm, ah... but... actually. Yes."

"You know, after seven years of vocal training, my Guru told me my swaram (musical tone) was just coming under control. How can you train my son to give a public concert in three months?"

"Amma, your son was very keen... I have six children to feed."

Mother gave him a fresh coconut, a brand new *veshti*, and one hundred and one rupees. He left, a nimbus cloud darkening his amicable face.

I emerged from behind the fridge.

To this day, I remain an everywhere musician without an audience – an uncut, unpolished diamond.

~

20

Police State – or Shangri-La?

It was with trepidation that I landed in Singapore last year, I was going to spend a lot of time there using it as a hub to visit places in South East Asia. Would I get into trouble in a country that has an authoritarian government and is reputed to be a police state? Is my big mouth going to let me down? Such was my state of mind when I stepped off the plane that anyone with a lanyard around their neck gave me the jitters. Everyone else, I feared, were police officers in *mufti!* Paranoid, if you want a one-word summary of my mental state. And ignorant, I hear some of you remark.

It took me a couple of days to realise that my fears were exaggerated. Yes, it's a small island with near-total CCTV surveillance. Its four pillars of democracy are not as robust as each other. But as long as I didn't jaywalk, spit in public places, molest, litter, or organise a political rally, no one was interested in me. As I don't habitually indulge in any of the above, jaywalking excepted, I was fine. I would be spared judicial caning both metaphorical and, for the most heinous of crimes and overstaying one's visa, literal! In any case, over 50s are exempt from caning, I have learned since.

It was only after I was disabused of this starkly negative imagination of Singapore that I started looking around to appreciate its charm. The order, cleanliness, the tension-free coexistence of three distinct races – Chinese, Malay, and Indian – were remarkable. So were the discipline and civic sense of ordinary people. As to places of touristic interest, I'll spare you the agony of my description and recommend you to refer to publicly available material.

My Indian–British conditioned mind did, however, lead me to a deeper question on the merits of Singaporean society. Some of us may find it difficult to reconcile with the idea of the nanny state telling us how to behave. Apparently, in 1980, Lord Balfour, a British politician, had vehemently opposed mandatory seatbelt legislation, calling it a nanny state intervention. He also worried about future legislation regarding lifejackets! (This piece of information from Wikipedia made me smile. During my tenure at the UK's Marine Accident Investigation Branch, I had written an entire report arguing for the wearing of lifejackets on small boats to be made mandatory.) While I make no argument in support of a nanny state, I am tempted to quote Lee Kuan Yew, the founding father of modern Singapore:

> *And I say without the slightest remorse, that we wouldn't be here, we would not have made economic progress, if we had not intervened on very personal matters – who your neighbour is, how you live, the noise you make, how you spit, or what language you use.*

I can't disagree with Mr Lee considering how since its separation from Malaysia in 1965, Singapore has transformed into one of the wealthiest and most peaceful nations on earth.

Confucius had said that all that is needed is a benevolent king who always acts in the best interest of his subjects. Singapore's perfect king, the People's Action Party, in power since the inception of the country, has enjoyed tremendous popularity and governs with a massive majority in parliament.

Home ownership is close to ninety percent. Indices of human development are what most developed countries can only dream about. Per capita share of the GDP is third in the world, crime is minimal, and justice almost instant. Yes, I can't march down the streets waving a flag, declaring my allegiance to a cause – unless I've taken prior permission to do so.

So, all things considered, would I live in Singapore? Absolutely, if they will have me. Would I bring up my children there? Well, in my book, a rounded education includes a bit of chaos, a touch of madness, and a sliver of defiance. So, no.

~

21

Wabi-Sabi in Penang

Georgetown, a UNESCO world heritage site on Penang Island, at the northwest coast of the Malay Peninsula, is a potpourri of cultures. Chinese, Malay, Indian, Siamese and the hybrid Peranakan traditions thrive in distinct but harmonious coexistence. The universality of the English language aids seamless communication within the population. European expatriates and tourists complete the backdrop.

Imposing but grand buildings with colonnades of pillars dating back to the colonial period keep a constant watch on the Strait of Malacca. Ancient and ubiquitous Angsana trees offer respite from the tropical heat. The trill of birds cuts through the jasmine-scented air of tranquil gardens. In the busier part of town, eateries offer cuisine that titillates the taste buds and makes one wish for a stomach of limitless capacity. And there is an abundance of cold beer to beat the sweltering heat.

Past and present merge seamlessly, their dichotomy subsumed by the charm of the town. One experiences both the then and now in equal measures. Quaint.

"It's a pity some of these walls are so old and run down," I remark to my cousin and travel companion as we explored the town and its street art including the famous wrought iron caricatures.

"Have you heard of *Wabi-Sabi*?" he asks. He is a committed Japanophile and derives inspiration for his creative work from the refined aesthetics of Japan and their art of graceful design.

"Oh, yes! I don't like it at all. It just hits me – feels like my brain is on fire," I responded.

He didn't call me a Philistine but clarified that he wasn't talking about wasabi, the horseradish purée that complements sushi, but Wabi-Sabi – the Japanese concept of beauty in impermanence, the acceptance of the transient nature of everything and elegance in imperfection. A completely new idea for me, a far cry from Singapore where every building resembles a wedding cake.

I studied the idea a little more and gave it serious thought. Somewhere along the way, this new concept altered the world around me. I began to see beauty despite the surface flaws, appreciate asymmetry, and respect the graceful ageing of things. I started observing the patina on a wall as adding to its charm instead of wanting to give it a good scrub and a lick of paint. Above all, Wabi-Sabi added a temporal elasticity to everything around and within me – both physical constructions and metaphysical abstractions like human relationships. It added a new dimension to my perception, a living continuum instead of a dead stillness. I changed a little.

~

22

Hearing Loss and Dementia

It started with an eye test. The eyes are fine, they told me, and haven't deteriorated in the past year. But would I be interested in a free hearing test?

"Fine," I said. "Let's do it." You see, I have a soft spot for freebies.

I went to the next room, and a young audiologist in his early thirties asked me if I suffered any hearing loss.

"Not really," I said, "although I can't hear the oven timer when I'm in the living room watching TV."

I had been using this particular handicap to my advantage. It's always my wife who pauses the TV and goes to check the pizza or whatever's in the oven. I just sit there, taking the opportunity to check my phone. Nevertheless, I would wonder why she used to keep disappearing. If I asked her, "Where are you going?" she just responded with a sad smile.

"Anything else?" the audiologist continued.

"No, except my wife sometimes complains that my hearing is going from bad to worse. But that's because she mumbles."

I could see a glint in his eye at the prospect of selling me a hearing aid.

"No problem. We'll soon find out," he said, handing me a set of headphones and starting up his computer. Long story short, I was told I had moderate hearing loss in my right ear, and after further tests involving progressively quieter monologues spoken in an American accent over heavy background noise, he confirmed – the glint in his eye now a steady glow – that my hearing could do with some 'assistance.' He wasn't using the dreaded *H* word yet. I knew the game was up for me. But I wasn't going to succumb so easily.

"So," I interrogated him, "what happens if I do nothing? Will my hearing get worse?"

"Your hearing will deteriorate, just as mine will, over the years. However, research has shown that uncorrected hearing loss leads to cognitive impairment," he replied with prophetic finality. He had me there. He was singing a requiem in honour of the last vestiges of my youth.

Sometimes it's better to appear to have lost the argument in order to gain a future advantage – like a chess gambit.

"Do you have a hearing aid I could try? And perhaps we could repeat some tests?" I asked tentatively.

He readily agreed and inserted a hearing aid in my right ear. However, he was selective in the tests he would repeat. He wouldn't replay the tests with the American accent but agreed to play some single words instead. I didn't like the hearing aid one bit. There was a delay in hearing my own speech. It felt as if someone was physically carrying the words from my mouth to my ears. Moreover, it sounded tinny, like a cheap old radio.

"We can see a 30% improvement," the audiologist finally informed me, pointing to his computer screen as evidence. But I had already made up my mind.

"No! I'm not having it," I delivered my verdict. Noticing the crestfallen expression on his face, I added with insincerity, "Let's give it another year."

I went in for an eye test and came out with visions of myself turning into a deaf, demented old geezer. That was the thought foremost in my head as I walked out of the shop. Nevertheless, I was damned if I would get a hearing aid.

The audiologist's prognosis weighed on my mind for a few days. But human beings are adept at getting rid of unpleasant memories, and I soon managed to forget all about the hearing aid affair.

A couple of weeks later, my wife and I went out for dinner with some friends. I only had a glass of wine with my meal, so inebriation can be ruled out for what followed. Back home, I retrieved my handkerchief from my right trouser pocket. When I got home, I slipped my hand into my right trouser pocket to take out my handkerchief. That's when I noticed something else – in the left pocket – a neatly folded table napkin from the restaurant!

An uncomfortable thought occurred to me. Is the audiologist's prophecy coming true?

~

23

The Clive Collection

(A shortened version, 'Their museum, my sighs', was published by The Times of India, 29 July 2025)

Our family holidays are invariably hard work. No basking in the sun with a book and a Margarita, no lie-in or breakfast in bed. Our days follow a regular 9 to 5 kind of routine with every obscure venue of the slightest historical significance visited, studied, and photographed. All our holidays have been to places steeped in history – the more ancient the better, ruins are mandatory and a skeleton or two is a bonus. I have navigated endless aisles in the Louvre, worn my shoes out in the Smithsonian, and am on a first name basis with the mummies of the British Museum. If you are married to a historian you will empathise with me.

There's always an exception to everything, something that breaks the pattern and makes life interesting. Our recent visit to Powys Castle in Wales to see the Clive Collection was one such outlier.

Powys Castle houses an impressive collection of Mughal era artefacts from India. The Clive Collection (Clive's loot to quote the well-known historian William Dalrymple) is a reminder of a murky period in history involving the East India Company who were masters of stealth, guile and deceit. But that is history and one shouldn't quarrel with history.

Sadly, photography in the castle is prohibited. So, you will have to bear with my thousand words instead. The most stunning display is one of the finials detached from the throne of Tipu Sultan of Mysore – a dazzlingly well-made tiger-head in solid gold studded with diamonds, rubies and emeralds. Other objects of importance are the ornately carved palanquin of Siraj-ud-Daulah, the last Nawab of Bengal; the elegant chintz cotton tent that Tipu Sultan used during his battles; delicately carved ivory chess pieces, almost weightless – one felt they would float away but for their encasements; and a multitude of other exquisite pieces outnumbering any collection in national museums across the subcontinent, including those of Afghanistan, Pakistan, India and Bangladesh.

I observed each object with an intensity I didn't know I possessed. It was as if my own history lay bare among the ivory hilted daggers and swords, the curved gold-brocaded shoes and the elaborate paintings. I was peeping into a time gone by, an epoch I had only learned about in school during dry, one-dimensional history lessons. I was unable to make sense of the affinity I felt towards the objects. It was like trying to remember the details of a vivid but elusive dream. Nevertheless, as I stood among Clive's collection that morning, I could hear the echo of battle cries and the neigh and stomping hooves of horses.

That evening as we drove home, I concluded that one could only enjoy a visit to a museum if there is a personal connection to the objects on display. I have decided not to visit another museum unless it ticks this box.

~

24

Munnar, Kerala

Munnar, a place of raw natural beauty, is situated in the Western Ghats some 5200 feet above sea level and only around a three-hour drive from Kochi. I visited the place with a friend from my student days. I wasn't concerned that it rained heavily and when it didn't, a thick fog obscured the idyllic charm of its undulating hills and tea plantations. Somehow, our conversation took precedence over the weather.

My friend was grappling with an existentialist question:

"Who am I and what is it that remains if I were to shed, layer by layer, everything that constitutes me?"

Sadly, I had grown old and had stopped pondering philosophical questions such as these. However, my interest was rekindled very quickly and we debated endlessly standing on the balcony, ignoring the thick fog within a few feet of us. The trill of invisible mountain birds gave us a sense of our location. We were aware of our surroundings, but only just.

As we tried to express in words what defies expression, the fog cleared partially showing us a glimpse of the delightful scenery beyond, a perfect metaphor for our conversation and its fleeting insights. The fog returned, matching our abstruse discussion with its opaqueness.

The strange thing was neither of us complained about not receiving full value for our money by way of missing out on the scenery. Each other's company and friendship were somehow sufficient to shine a beam of bright sunlight through the low-lying cloud.

~

25

Secrets

Once there lived a king who had the ears of a donkey. They were long and furry and stood up straight from the side of his head. No one except the royal barber knew.

The king deftly hid it under a turban that was never removed. Even the queen wasn't aware of his secret – he kept his turban on at all times. The barber was warned that he would pay with his head if he so much as breathed the secret to anyone.

The knowledge of the king's donkey ears weighed the barber down like an anchor. He had to tell someone but knew the consequences would be dire if he did. He was on the verge of losing his mind. One day he had a bright idea. He planted the sapling of a mahogany tree in a remote corner of his compound, watered it and screamed to his heart's content.

"Hear this! Hear this! The king has donkey ears, the king has donkey ears ... hahaha ... hohoho."

He experienced immense relief after this. He breathed easy once again. The king's secret no longer bothered him and he lived happily for many years.

One day, the wedding of the princess was announced. The entire country celebrated the build-up, with much feasting and rejoicing. Soldiers visited once, looking for suitable wood with which to make drums. They spotted the fully grown mahogany tree in the barber's compound, chopped it down and delivered it to the royal drum makers.

As the wedding garlands were being exchanged and the drum beats reached a crescendo, the voice of the barber rang out loud and clear:

"The king has donkey ears, the king has donkey ears ... hahaha ... hohoho."

The king was a man of his word. Hence, this story sadly ends with a headless barber.

I'm in a similar situation as the barber. My head is about to burst with secrets. I have been told far too many in the last two weeks. They're weighing me down – the knowledge of terrible insinuations being made about some people, the diseases that some are battling with, impending divorces, extra-marital and pre-marital affairs...

However, I'm not allowed to tell anyone. I've been sworn to secrecy; my honour is at stake. And the more honourable I am, the more sordid the secrets I receive.

Please don't tell me anything more. I am full up. And if you find it hard to keep them, go plant a tree and confide in it. Kings are not allowed to behead you these days.

~

26

The Pacer

The one good thing about COVID was it required us to exercise once a day. Most of us looked forward to the one hour outing we were allowed every day, and my wife and I were no exception. However, there was a problem. My wife liked to walk slowly, admiring the wild plants and ducks. I liked to walk as if I were about to miss a flight. The result? I would be far ahead, waiting for her while she ambled along like traffic during rush hour on the M25.

"Walk faster," I would entreat her.

"You walk fast if you want," she would retort.

It is no use arguing with her. She tends to dig her heels in, the more persuasive I become. One day, we had some minor disagreement that turned into a full-blown argument. The curious thing was, as long as we were arguing, she kept pace with me, matching me step for step, word for word. That's when I had my epiphany.

From the next day onwards, five minutes into our walk, I would start a small argument – nothing to do with household matters or with the potential to escalate, but something that held tremendous promise for an hour's worth of harmless disagreement. So, for instance, keeping a deadpan expression, I would say something like,

"How can anyone live on the South Pole? Won't they be standing upside down?"

She would look at me as if I had completely lost it and respond, "I can't believe this. Just what are you saying? Have you heard of gravity?"

"Yes, but gravity only makes sure you don't fall off into space. But you'll still be upside down."

"So you think the Antarcticans are all upside down?" she would try sarcasm.

"Yes, exactly! Imagine an ant going round a football. However big the football, by the time it reaches the bottom of the ball, it would be upside down. No? It's simple logic. Think about it..."

"OMG! What's the matter with you?" she would move from incredulous to mildly amused to slightly irritated.

"It may sound silly, but actually, it's not," and so on I would string it along, gradually increasing my pace all the while.

She would match my pace while trying to drum some sense into my head. And so it would continue until we returned home. Back at our front door, I would admit defeat and declare, "Yes. You're right."

And all would be well once more.

~

27

Ganesh Chaturthi and the Coconut Problem

Ganesh Chaturthi is the birthday of the elephant-headed god Ganesha. There is an interesting story behind his creation. Even more interesting was how Ganesha solved my coconut problem once.

Parvati, the consort of Lord Shiva, was alone at home while Shiva spent aeons in deep meditation in the Himalayas. Feeling vulnerable and wishing for a companion, she created a boy out of clay and ghee, gave him life, and began treating him as her son. One day, she went to bathe in the river, instructing the boy to keep guard and not let anyone pass. As she was bathing, Shiva came to visit and made his way to the river. However, the boy did not let him pass despite his demands to be let through. Angered by his obduracy, Shiva cut off the boy's head. He then went to find Parvati. She was deeply upset when informed of the murder of her son and started venting her anger at her husband. Feeling contrite, he promised her that he would replace the boy's head with the head of the first living creature he encounters. An elephant was passing by. So, Shiva promptly took its head and installed it on the boy. He was named Ganesha, meaning king of elephants. And everyone lived happily ever after, except, of course, half the elephant.

Ganesha or Ganapathy is also called Vighneshwara – the god who removes obstacles. Hindus across India worship

Ganesha for this quality. People perform special *puja*, ritualistic worship, when they start a new venture. Almost every Hindu home, shop, car, tuktuk, motorcycle, briefcase, wallet... has a little idol or image of Ganesha. Such is the faith reposed in him. Although born a Hindu, I don't practise the religion – either overtly or covertly. But that day I had a problem, and I like to believe Ganesha solved it for me.

My wife asked me to get some vegetables including a coconut so she could make a feast for Ganesh Chaturthi. I went to a nearby shop, but they had run out of coconuts. So, I returned home with a bag full of vegetables but no coconut. Now, if you know South Indian cuisine, you'll understand the gravity of this omission.

Coconut is an essential ingredient – it is the potato in jacket potato, the milk in latte, the cream in strawberries and cream. It plays a major role in flavouring, garnishing, and seasoning vegetables. It is also used to make traditional sweets during Ganesh Chaturthi. So yes, coming home without one was a culinary catastrophe. My wife was not pleased. Fortunately, unlike young Ganesha before his makeover, I kept my head. Eventually, we were reconciled to make do without coconut. This is when my wife scalded her finger in the kitchen. I was dispatched once again to get some *Burnol*.

After purchasing the ointment, I decided to take a different route back home. Then I noticed a little Ganesha temple constructed on the pavement. It was a fully functioning temple, complete with two priests, a fine idol of Ganesha, garlands of flowers, lamps and bells. Let me collect some *prasad* for my elderly mother-in-law, I thought. I stood in front of the idol and folded my hands in supplication. The priest waved a copper plate brimming with marigold and hibiscus flowers, burning oil lamps in little clay pots, sindoor (vermilion) and holy ashes above and around my head, and chanted a prayer in Sanskrit asking Vighneshwara to remove the obstacles in my path. It was a scene rich with scent and symbolism. The smell of burning camphor and warm coconut oil wafted towards me from the idol, and there I was – for all practical purposes a devout Hindu like any other, paying obeisance to the Remover of Obstacles. I accepted the prasad – the remnants of the offering presented to the gods. Hidden among the flowers, the sweets, and the vermilion was half a coconut.

It wasn't just an offering – it was a propitious sign. Perhaps trivial, perhaps serendipitous. But in that moment, I chose to believe that Ganesha had done what he does best: removed an obstacle from my path.

Shiva is known as *'The Destroyer'* or *'The Transformer'* within the Hindu trinity. His role complements that of **Brahma**, who creates the universe, and **Vishnu**, who preserves it. Shiva destroys not in a purely negative sense, but to enable regeneration and renewal – a necessary step in the cosmic cycle.

~

28

Mahashankh (The Great Conch Shell)

A story told by 'Bhagwan' Rajneesh sticks in my mind. Those of my vintage will remember the controversial 'Sex Guru'.

A man did years of tapasya (penance through deep meditation) until God appeared briefly one night. He gave him a *shankh* (conch shell) and said that all he had to do was blow into it and ask for anything. The man did as instructed. A voice from the shankh announced,

"I am at your service, master. Ask for anything."

The man asked for a kilogram of gold. A block of gold materialised instantly. Just like that! Before the night was out, he had ordered everything he ever wanted and more. His simple thatched hut was replaced by an opulent palace. Luxury cars with liveried chauffeurs lined up outside, an army of servants ran around attending to him, and a complete harem of desirable women frolicked in his perfumed gardens. It was as if a celestial branch of Harrods had opened in his backyard, and everything, including delivery, was free. Soon, he ran out of ideas on things to order.

One day, a roaming mendicant came to his palace and said to him,

"I hear you have a shankh that gives you everything you want?"

"Yes, yes!" replied our man.

"I have a *Mahashankh*. It'll give you double of everything

you ask."

Our man, greedy and stupid in equal measure, asked if he could buy it. But the mendicant replied,

"I have no use for money. But if you want, we could exchange our shankhs."

It was a no-brainer. Stupid mendicant, he thought, and quickly gave up his shankh and received a much larger one in return.

The man blew into the Mahashankh, and a deep voice came from within it,

"Command me, and I'll give you double of what you want."

He said, "Give me a diamond."

Mahashankh said, "I'll give you two."

He waited patiently, but nothing happened. No diamond was delivered.

Maybe he had been misunderstood, he thought, and blew again.

"Yes, master, what can I do for you?"

"Where are the two diamonds you promised?"

"I'll give you four," said Mahashankh.

Nothing was delivered. Not even a pebble.

A bit impatient, our man blew a third time, and when asked how he could be served, he said rather impatiently,

"I'm still waiting for those four diamonds."

"I will give you eight," replied Mahashankh.

But it gave nothing.

This story had a profound effect on me when I heard it as a young man. To this day, I am terrified of making a promise I can't keep. If in the unlikely event that I haven't done something I said I would, please remind me. I don't want to be known as a Mahashankh.

~

29

An Onam Present From Mahabali

King Mahabali ruled Kerala once upon a time. He was a kind, benevolent ruler adored by the people. One day, the gods, jealous of his popularity, complained to the sustainer of the universe, Mahavishnu. Mahabali was usurping their elevated status among the people of Kerala, they said. He needed to be taught a lesson, pulled down a peg or two. Vishnu acceded to their demand. He transformed himself into a *vamana* (dwarf) and approached Mahabali,

"Great king, please grant me some land to meditate," he pleaded, "all I need is a plot covering three steps."

Mahabali immediately granted him his wish. No sooner had he said yes, than the vamana transformed into a giant – feet on the ground, head among the stars. With one step he covered the earth, with the next he took the heavens.

"Where shall I take the third step?" he roared.

Mahabali bowed down and indicated his head. As he was being pushed into the netherworld, Vishnu asked him if he had a last wish. Mahabali said he would like to visit his people once a year. Thus he emerges every year to spend ten days with his subjects. The occasion called Onam is the biggest festival of Kerala.

People of Kerala welcome their beloved king with floral decorations adorning floors. They offer him a grand and sumptuous lunch. Women put on their finest jewellery and everyone wears new clothes. Caparisoned elephants decked in flowers are paraded on the streets to the beat of drums and trumpets. Snake boats are raced in the backwaters. It is as if the people of Kerala genuinely believe that their favourite king has returned to them. The festivities last ten days, with people of all religions participating.

I was born in Kerala and spent my early childhood there. Some close relatives were staying with us in Southampton during this Onam season. It was perhaps bravura induced by a glass or two of celebratory rosé. I promised our guests that I would prepare the Onasadhya or Onam feast. They were excited by the prospect of a 27 item feast – yes you read that right – 27, all freshly cooked vegetarian dishes, served on banana leaves.

The enormity of my promise dawned on me the next day after the rosé had worn off. I had never cooked more than four items in a day. Yes, some of the 27 included banana chips (bought in a packet) and papadom which only has to be fried in oil. However, everything else needed to be cooked, vegetables diced, mustard seeds spluttered, coconut ground and its milk extracted, lentils soaked, and a hundred other operations carried out with precision and sequenced correctly to produce the goods. I would have to multitask, juggling the activities expertly if I wished to finish in time. To top it all, I didn't have a clue if all the traditional Onam vegetables could be purchased in Southampton. Where was I to find raw plantains and ash gourd and Kerala cucumber? What about banana leaves?

After a lot of nail biting and a few frantic calls to Malayali friends in Southampton, I obtained the address of a shop that sold the Onam paraphernalia. But I had to be quick because there are many other subjects of Mahabali in Southampton and all of them would be embarking on similar cooking projects.

My wife and I, with our two guests (our cousins) headed straight to the Kerala store. The shop was like an Aladdin's cave of exotic vegetables and groceries. Picking up a basket and holding a list that ran into several notebook pages, I started collecting the items one by one. As the basket filled, a part of me was rejoicing in sweet nostalgia and another major part was silently panicking.

And it was then that the cousin shouted across to me from the far corner of the shop as if she had found a treasure.

"Look, look," she said, pointing at some boxes in the freezer section. And there it was. Its label, Kerala vegetarian sadhya for five." The box contained 19 items, all individually packed and frozen. I only had to cook the rice (item 20), fry the papadom and defrost everything else. It was as if Mahabali, sensing the distress I was in, came up with a solution. I abandoned my basket, nostalgia and all, and grabbed a box.

We had to use some imagination to fill the remaining slots to get to the magic number of 27. So we added rosé, Chardonnay, gin and tonic, vodka and orange juice, and somewhere along the way lost the ability to count. We raised our glasses and proposed a toast to Mahabali, our very own king cheated by some jealous gods.

~

30

Punctured Pride

Until last week, I never believed I had grown old. I thought I was around 40 – not a day older. But a punctured cycle tyre deflated me and convinced me that I am indeed an old geezer. Although I managed to fix the cycle tyre, I doubt if I can ever repair my punctured self-image.

The day started well. My friend S and I took the 0900 Red Jet from Southampton to the Isle of Wight, getting there in a mere 30 minutes. Shortly, we were on the Red Squirrel cycle track – a 32 mile traffic-free off-road route passing estuaries, meadows and woodlands. Originally an old steam train track, it's a delightful journey into another world, a rustic countryside untouched as yet by the ravages of climate change or greedy builders, resonating with the songs of curlews and dissonant shrieks of gulls. We stopped to eat sweet wild apples and I even tasted a berry that looked like an apple.

A few miles later, just before Sandown, we had lunch. Feeling satiated and content with the world, we set off again. Then it happened – the cyclist's nemesis, a puncture, got me. The sinking feeling experienced when the wheel rim makes hard contact with the track. For a few fleeting seconds, one's world comes to an end. There's nothing to live for. The black hole of depression swallows you whole.

This is when a good cycling mate comes in handy. S was not perturbed and remained equanimous.

"No worries," he reassured me. I turned the bike upside

down and dismantled the wheel. The next step was to remove the tyre; our plastic tyre levers were not up to the job. It was like the tyre was three sizes smaller. Eventually, we got it out but couldn't put it back on after changing the inner tube. I was going from tired to exhausted to fatigued, and my back was screaming blue murder. I would have given up if I had the choice. A passing cyclist, in the spirit of camaraderie between cyclists, offered his tyre levers and the stubborn tyre was finally back in place.

My portable pump struggled to build up the required pressure and it occurred to us that the café we lunched at might have a track pump. And they did. They had metal levers too, and if only we had thought of it earlier we would've saved ourselves a lot of angst. But then we had already made several assumptions.

That's the imperfect way we live our lives – jumping to conclusions, making general inferences based on scant data, second guessing how the other person would react ... By the time I was back on the road, I felt like I had run a marathon after a trans-continental flight. All I did was fix a puncture. I must have grown old while I wasn't watching!

~

31

Waking up from Hibernation

I thought I had retired. But apparently some think I haven't. So, when asked by a friend if I would do an accident investigation, the only question I asked was, "Where?" to which he replied,

"Valencia, Spain."

That sealed the deal. Ever since I sailed on a ship with a Chilean crew some decades ago, I have had this obsession with mastering conversational Spanish. I learned the rudiments of the language and could communicate with a bit of effort. In life, one is defined by self-perception. It's a bit like the people who think they can sing. Negative comments don't register with them because they think you're talking about someone else. Similarly, I used to think I spoke good Spanish. People were generally encouraging and told me how good I was, although as I improved my comprehension, I also understood occasional comments such as, "He speaks a bit of Spanish." That hurt, of course, but overall I never let my self-image suffer any major blows.

I also used to think I was good at French. But that story ended in tears...

I spent a year on a reefer ship that sailed between Marseille in France and the ports of French-speaking countries in West Africa including Senegal, Ivory Coast, and Cameroon. Reefer is jargon for refrigerated cargo and not what some of you Bob Marley fans might be thinking. I thought it was a great opportunity to become proficient in French. Purchasing a French Linguaphone set of books and cassette tapes, I spent my free hours at sea studying and practising my skills on innocent strangers in ports. Thanks to the delicate nature of our cargo, loading and discharging were relatively slow and our ship enjoyed long port stays. I got ample opportunities to practise.

I would walk up to random people and ask them directions for places I had no intention of visiting, and visit restaurants to order food and drinks even though I wasn't hungry. I got my kicks from the interaction, the feeling of satisfaction that I could communicate in French, that people could understand me. I felt I was only a few steps away from reading Voltaire and Rousseau in the original French. In short, my self-concept was running way ahead of reality. Until the day my illusions were shattered while travelling in a taxi in Abidjan with three shipmates.

I sat in the front and my colleagues were squashed in the back seat. I spoke in French to the driver who just kept nodding his head, interjecting with the occasional, 'oui, oui.' I kept going, regurgitating everything I had taught myself, telling him about the weather, commenting on the places I liked in his country, Côte d'Ivoire, filling him in on my family details, the food I liked... totally unconnected and disparate topics but which were part of the Linguaphone lessons I had already mastered. In short, I was just showing off to my colleagues who sat quietly with open-mouthed admiration writ large upon their faces. After patiently suffering me for over ten minutes, the driver suddenly let go of both hands from the steering wheel of the running car, turned his face to me and, crossing his forearms like an X, said, "STOP – s'il vous plaît – STOP. Me – I no understand your English!"

My colleagues had the evening of their lives talking to me in broken French and frequently crossing their arms and screaming, "STOP s'il vous plaît!" They never let me forget the episode to the day I signed off the ship. When the ship sailed out late that night, I gave a solemn sea burial to the Linguaphone programme. And that was the end of my liaison with the French language.

That was a side story. The sooner I forget it the better. I have more positive memories of my attempts to learn Spanish. As said earlier, it started with a ship where most of the crew was from Chile. I was one of three Indians aboard. The conversation around the dinner table was in Spanish and I felt excluded. My ship called at most ports in Chile from Punta Arenas in Patagonia to the desert of Iquique near the Peruvian border. We also called at ports in Peru, Ecuador, Colombia, and every other South American country that was not landlocked. Spanish is spoken everywhere except in Brazil. It was imperative that I learned Spanish if I wanted to get the pulse of the peoples of South America.

So, one day I told Sergio Gijado, the motorman (a colleague who assists the engineer on watch in the engine room), to speak to me only in Spanish and also to teach me some grammar. When the ship called at Valparaíso, Sergio's home port, he brought me some grammar books. I made very good progress. Sergio was an excellent teacher, correcting my grammar, adding a few words to my vocabulary every day and unravelling the complexities of the sixteen Spanish tenses, all in the comfort of the engine control room.

Once, we had overhauled an engine unit in port – pulled out the piston, calibrated the cylinder liner and replaced the piston with an overhauled one. Those who have been to sea will know that everything aboard has to be secured properly, unless you want things flying about during rough seas. I was on watch when the ship sailed out, and Sergio was assisting me. As soon as we cleared the breakwaters, the ship started rolling, gently at first and quite heavily after a short while. Sergio was taking his rounds in the engine room but soon he burst into the control room shouting in Spanish,

"Señor, el pistón se está cayendo."

I figured out something was happening to the piston – but I did not know what, because cayendo was not in my Spanish lexicon. Sergio was normally a calm person, rarely perturbed by anything. However, the panic on his face was palpable. So I too panicked without really knowing why. I tried asking him in English what happened. But he continued answering in Spanish. Finally, I shook him by his shoulders and screamed at him.

"Sergio, speak English! ¡Habla inglés por favor!"

"Señor," he said, pointing in the direction of the engine room, "the piston – he is falling down."

We ran to the cylinder head platform and what I saw then still wakes me up in cold sweat at night. We had forgotten to clamp the old piston in its place. The massive cast iron piston with a crown nearly a metre in diameter, attached to a piston rod two to three metres long and altogether weighing a couple of tonnes, was about to slip from its pedestal on the bulkhead and fall onto the running engine! I immediately summoned more help and eventually we managed to clamp it in place.

But that experience only strengthened my resolve to improve my vocabulary. By the time I signed off that vessel,

I was reasonably fluent in Spanish and Sergio continued to speak only Spanish to me until my last day aboard.

So, that was the *alaap* – an introductory prelude. Now you know why I came out of retirement, willingly. In the next story, I hope to narrate my experiences in Valencia.

~

32

Valencia

My first emotion on landing in Valencia was mild disappointment. On the signboards in the airport, everything was repeated in three languages. The first line was in a language similar to Spanish, the next was English, and then proper Spanish. I guessed the first language could be Catalan, spoken in Barcelona and other places in Catalonia. It was a bit like an Indian railway station where the signboards have the first line in the local language, then Hindi – the presumed national language, although we Southies resent this imposition, and finally English.

I ignored the Catalan – known locally as Valencian – and concentrated only on the español. Walking from the plane to passport control, I picked up a few new words. Heaps of old ones, tucked away in obscure crannies of my brain, emerged with gusto. It was blissfully refreshing – like the smell of first rain on parched land, like finding some long-lost heirloom behind the cupboard. My Spanish proficiency was travelling back to me through the intervening decades with reckless speed.

The taxi driver who was engaged to take me to the hotel was called Alexandro (he pronounced x like a hard h, like the Spanish *j: Alehandro).* He started talking to me in laborious English. When I replied in even more laborious Spanish, he was well pleased and didn't need any encouragement to switch languages. He started rattling away in Spanish at breakneck speed. I pleaded with him to slow down, "Despacio, por favor."

Then he calmed down and spoke deliberately and slowly. I understood most of what he said. What a warm feeling it was. Old forgotten phrases came alive and danced in the air like cherubs. It's intriguing how a language comes back to you when you're immersed in the environment.

Alexandro told me he was from Argentina. I promptly endeared myself to him further by telling him of my visit to the port of Rosario and my day trip to Buenos Aires from there. I told him how a complete stranger had invited me to a cocktail party, and I then extrapolated generously to how I thought the Argentinians were a hospitable lot. It's always unwise to generalise, but when it's complimentary generalisation, it could work in one's favour.

Alexandro asked me if I liked living in the UK. I said, "Sí, me encanta!" (Yes, I love it!). Then he told me about his uncle who had fought in the Falklands War. Apparently, his uncle was captured as a POW, but the Brits fed him better than the Argentinian army ever did. I was glad someone was speaking well of my home, considering the world thinks it fashionable to knock America and Britain.

By the time we reached the hotel, he and I had shared details about our respective families and exchanged personal telephone numbers. I had a best friend in Valencia.

When one visits a place as a tourist, one is well informed about it. YouTube videos, Wikipedia articles and ChatGPT are studied and consulted. However, when the visit is related to work, this is rarely the case. I was engrossed in the details of the accident, worried about the challenges of conducting a thorough investigation in one day, and was generally preoccupied with the logistics of the job. I knew nothing about Valencia.

So, when after breakfast I took a stroll outside, not expecting to see anything extraordinary, the sight of the most creative structures ever built – the set of buildings known collectively as *La Ciudad de las Artes y las Ciencias* (The City of Arts and Sciences) – took my breath away. Built on the bed of a river that was drained and diverted due to past flooding, these were extraordinarily elegant and ingenious in construction. Some of them appeared weightless!

I walked around clicking my phone like photography was going out of fashion. Usually, I don't do selfies. I have a view on selfies, perhaps to be expanded on another occasion. Nevertheless, that morning, I wanted to be immortalised among the magical buildings. I handed my phone to a stranger and requested him to take my picture. Maybe I got the Spanish wrong, or perhaps the man was psychic and became aware of my aversion to selfies. On examining the pictures he took, I observed that I was not included in any of the pictures.

"Muchas gracias, ¿pero dónde estoy?" I said. (Thank you very much, but where am I?)

He seemed surprised and gave me a look that said, 'Make up your mind, mate!' He then took a couple of pictures with me in it.

The ship arrived around 11 a.m. I was on board soon after and only completed my work late in the evening. The driver who transported me back to the hotel was from Uruguay. I was exhausted – mentally and physically. There was no energy left for further gymnastics with Spanish. We spoke in English, and I reminisced about the time my wife and I visited the lovely capital city of Uruguay, Montevideo. I made another best friend in Valencia.

"Buenas noches, Martín," I wished the Uruguayan driver good night and, within an hour, fell asleep in my room.

The next morning, after securely filing away all the electronic evidence from the ship, I had exactly four free hours before the taxi ride back to the airport. But that must wait until the next story.

~

33

The Invisible Light

(A shortened version, 'Northern Lights Illusion', was published by The Times of India, 14 April 2025)

If someone should show you their selfie with the northern lights, ask them straight away if they actually saw them. This is a question that challenges our fundamental understanding of what it means to see. Any honest person worth their salt would think twice before responding to this question.

Allow me to narrate a side story. You'll soon see the connection.

Back in 2017, we had a class reunion at Corbett National Park in Kumaon, the foothills of the Himalayas. We had organised a safari in the forest starting at 5 a.m. Except for a handful of those who valued their sleep over tiger sighting, most of us braved the cold morning and boarded the 4x4s organised for us. All the vehicles took different routes into the forest so as not to generate too much noise and scare away the animals. We spent hours trawling the forest, but saw nothing – no tiger, no elephant, not even a wild boar. We did see a couple of stray dogs, but they were hardly wild. The animals had decided to boycott us and we came back tired, hungry and feeling rather foolish. I noticed a classmate walking around with a swagger while the rest of us moped about, shoulders slumped.

I asked my smiling friend, “Looks like you saw a tiger?”

“No. But I saw a man who saw a tiger,” he replied. I couldn’t help a sarcastic jibe and asked him if he got a photo of the man.

“Oh no! I forgot to do that,” he said, a rueful expression darkening his naïve, innocent face.

On a similar vein, if you ask me whether I have seen the northern lights, I will look at you shifty-eyed, squirm in my seat and reply,

“Well, I have a camera that saw it.”

So here is the rub. A couple of years ago in the month of February, my wife and I visited Tromsø at the northern tip of Norway. We braved the cold, broke the bank, and dressed like mummies. Every inch of skin was protected from the cold howling wind by several layers of thermals and woollens. We travelled in a small van with some others, our flasks brimming with hot cocoa, our hearts brimming with hope. The tour guide regaled us with warm Scandinavian stories and reassured us that the northern lights, when they do appear in the sky, would be a life-changing experience for us. It did happen yesterday, he assured us, and it happens almost every night – so long as it doesn’t rain or snow. Then he said something that intrigued me. Looking up at the sky through the windscreen, he said, “There’s a Scandinavian saying – ‘All cats look grey at night. ’”

I didn’t understand the relevance then but I was soon to find out.

The night was clear, stars canopied the sky, and the van was toasty. The street lights gradually disappeared as we sped out of town into eerie darkness. Finally we stopped. Except for the black tarmac of the road everything was white. There was no moon, just starlight reflecting off the snow. And there was snow everywhere, fresh snow like icing on a cake.

We were asked not to use any flashlights or use the flash on our cameras because our eyes had to get used to the low light. So we trudged along the snow fields, further and further away from the road until we reached a dip in the valley, where we waited ... and waited ... multiple mittens and socks and boots and balaclavas kept us fairly warm for a while but the cold eventually prevailed. We wriggled our toes and fingers to make sure they were still attached. Like astronauts on the moon we walked about aimlessly, necks craned upwards and talking in hushed whispers until someone told us we don't have to whisper!

Then, "There it is," the guide pointed heavenward at a large bright white streak across the sky.

I could detect a forced ring of enthusiasm in his voice. The tourists, though inwardly disappointed, joined in, "Wow! How lovely!" They echoed the guide's half-hearted cheer.

I'm someone who wants value for money. I didn't travel to the North Pole to see a glorified cloud. I wanted to see the full spectrum or at least a hint of it.

"But I only see white," I complained. I had said what everyone else was too polite to say.

"Yes, yes," the guide said. "As we grow older, we don't see colours too well."

So it was my fault! I looked around. Turning my head in their general direction, I asked, "Can anyone see any colour?"

All the mummies shook their heads. The guide was

defeated. He then came up with his next trick. Erecting a tripod on the snow, he invited me to fix my camera and adjust it to a very slow shutter speed, a high ISO setting and a few other settings I never even knew existed. Then he asked my wife and me to pose with the northern whites, sorry lights, behind us and told us to stay still. We were already semi frozen, so it was not difficult to follow his instructions. He remote released the shutter and it took its time while we stood unflinching and unbreathing. He finally approached us with a broad smile combing icicles off his beard and returned my camera with a flourish.

"Have a look!" he said, smiling triumphantly.

And there it was, the Northern Lights in all their glory. A brilliant emerald green tinged with blues and yellows instead of the white streak. He repeated the exercise with all the tourists. We returned to our respective hotels clutching our cameras that had seen the Northern Lights.

(P.S. The next day we saw the Northern Lights with naked eyes. It was a very brief *darshan*[6].)

~

6 *Darshan, a divine or spiritual sighting*

34

Umme Farah

A young girl with an endearing smile turned around in her seat and handed us a shiny new iPhone.

"Please take my photo when I go up on stage," she said to my wife. My wife agreed and seamlessly passed the phone on to me. I accepted it, primarily because I had no choice but also because the girl's strong subcontinental accent somehow reminded me of my student days in India. I had developed a soft spot for her.

All the above happened in a few seconds, and at one level it was no different to a stranger on the street asking for her picture to be taken. But under the circumstances, she had plunged us into a logistical nightmare.

We were at Cardiff University to attend the convocation ceremony for our son's postgraduate degree. I was my family's official photographer. I held a phone in one hand and balanced a regular camera on my chest with its zoom lens protruding like a periscope from my belly. We were sitting in one of the back rows some fifty metres from the stage. Everyone wore identical gowns and mortar boards. It was hard enough to recognise one's own son at that distance.

What chance did I have of identifying a total stranger? What if I missed her and didn't manage to get a proper photo? How disappointed would she be? How was she going to explain the total absence of photographs or videos to her parents in distant India or Pakistan? What a responsibility I had taken on. I completely forgot that I was there for my son and, instead, worried entirely about her. My son's graduation ceremony had become a sideshow!

"What's your name?"

"Farah."

I started scanning the printed graduation booklet for 'Sarah'. Pages and pages of names, mostly non-British. But no, Sarah, no, Jane, no, Sally. Nothing.

"I can't find you in the list," I told her with some concern, "No Sarah."

"Farah, not Sarah! FARAH with an F. Umme Farah," she said, a fleeting shadow of regret already clouding her face for asking me to be her official photographer. A simple task, she was probably thinking, made complicated by this geezer. But I was focused on the job. I needed to be able to identify this young woman from a distance among hundreds like her.

My retired accident investigator's hat came back on. I made mental notes of her prominent distinguishing features. Colour of hair – black, complexion – wheatish, as they say back in India, white leather skirt ... it was only when I got up from my seat to study her legs beyond her ankle-length skirt that my wife elbowed me in my ribs. Between being winded and sitting back down, I observed her shoes: black patent leather stilettos. Meanwhile, Umme Farah was trying to curl up into a small ball in her seat, the clouds of regret for engaging me in the role now settling decidedly on her face. She gave me a weak smile. I could read her mind. It declared, "OMG! What have I got myself into?"

I had enough data on her by then. I should be able to

identify her from where I was sitting. I would be able to look Umme Farah's parents in the eye if ever I met them. Then another doubt assailed me and I was back to chewing fingernails.

Would I be able to hear her name announced by the senior academic who was at times struggling with the vast array of foreign names? There were scores of Lees followed by Lius followed by Mas, hundreds of Mohammeds, a few dozen Guptas and Aggarwals and Venkatachalams interspersed among multitudes of Xis and Yus and Zhaos. I was reminded of the time when a lecturer in the South Tyneside technical college once called my classmate Submaranian instead of Subramanian. How many others were suffering a similar fate? Would he get Farah's name wrong? Would I therefore miss it?

I was however mildly comforted by the fact that the professor was also switching between English and fluent Welsh. In my opinion, a Welsh speaker has the capacity to handle any language. If someone can wrap their tongue around,

"Rhowch yr holl sbwriel mewn biniau wedi'u darparu" when he means,

"Put your rubbish in the bins provided," he is capable of saying anything with exactitude. Umme Farah would be a piece of Welsh cake for him.

And so it was. He pronounced her name with perfect diction, as her mother probably calls her. Farah appeared on stage doffing her hat to the vice chancellor and waving in our direction. I had her phone camera on video mode and recorded the entire episode without a glitch. I could hear myself shouting over the clapping and cheering.

"Brava, Brava, Umme Farah!"

I had forgotten the video would preserve every syllable for posterity. Decades hence, her grandchildren would listen with awe to my screams of encouragement. Reflecting on it later, I realised that my extra loud, throaty cries of felicitations for the young woman were really self-congratulatory. They expressed my immense relief for not messing up the Umme Farah project. And yes, my son's big moment was recorded on the camera – just about.

~

35

The Rope–Snake Conundrum

"When you see a rope and jump back in fear, mistaking it for a snake, where did the rope go?"

The question above was posed by Guru Freddy, formerly Fredrick van der Borght, a shipyard engineer from Belgium-turned guru, as we took a long walk through the city of Mysore in the summer of 1983. The thought did occur to me then that the question made no sense. However, my life's conditioning did not permit me to challenge the wisdom of a guru. In addition, he was my father's client. After years of struggle, Swami, later Guru, Freddy had managed to gain Indian citizenship. My father was his lawyer. That's the background. But why am I raking all this up now?

Three recent incidents made me rethink what Guru Freddy said to me some 40 years ago.

1 – On Monday, I attended a Pilates lesson at my local gym. As I returned to my recently acquired car, I noticed a large scratch on the front passenger side bumper. The parking bay to the damaged side was empty. The perpetrator had fled the scene. I stood there fuming, hollering vile expletives at the empty parking bay. Then I looked more closely at my damaged car. It was the same steel grey colour but it was not mine. It was not even the same make. On that day, my usual spot was taken and so I had parked elsewhere!

2 – I work with a voluntary organisation teaching English to asylum seekers living in Southampton. I'm also the visitor

for an Iranian man – call him Ahmed. A 'visitor' is like a local guardian or friend who would step in and help when necessary. It could be to assist with registering with the doctor's surgery, deal with a solicitor, write letters to the authorities and so on. Ahmed relies on my support.

Entering the building last Friday, I scanned the bustling throng of asylum seekers for Ahmed, but he was missing. His friend Mohsen was sitting around a table with some others. I asked him, "Where's Ahmed today?"

"He died yesterday," replied Mohsen.

"Died?" I felt weak, like someone had punched me in the gut.

Overwhelmed by the news, I muttered some incoherent remarks and finally managed, "But ... but how?"

"I don't know," Mohsen said with a shrug.

The conversation went back and forth for a minute or so. Then I saw Mohsen smile. It was a prank – his idea of a joke.

3 – Wednesday this week, I was relaxing in bed after a gruelling cycle ride. I was looking at something on the phone and a text message came in from my GP surgery.

"Dear Mr Chandroth, This is a reminder for your appointment at 17:20 ..."

I didn't read further. It was 17:15. I had five minutes to do the ten-minute journey. If not, I'll have to wait months before I get another appointment. Jumping out of bed, I changed my clothes and ran to my car in my flip-flops. Driving like a maniac, I got there by 17:25. I ran to the check-in computer, entered my date of birth, etc., but instead of confirming, it simply said, "Cannot find your appointment."

I had missed it. I was too late. My memory is like a sieve these days. Damn! I then read the message again.

"Dear Mr Chandroth, This is a reminder for your appointment at 17:20 tomorrow."

Thinking about the three incidents, I had an epiphany: there was actually no difference between reality and perception. The damaged car, the death of Ahmed and the missed doctor's appointment were real. The undamaged car, the live Ahmed and the next day's appointment did not exist. They – like the rope that turned into a snake – had disappeared and substituted themselves with alternatives.

While it is true that the new realities existed only briefly, it doesn't take away from the fact that every emotion I felt during those moments was genuine. What if the moments had stretched to a few hours or even days? What if you never realised the snake was, after all, just a piece of rope? Do we all experience versions of reality?

I posed the rope–snake conundrum to a friend. She in turn asked me a question that has very serious implications:

"What if you saw a snake and thought it was a rope?"

~

36

To Ask or Not to Ask

There are two types of cyclists. One who asks strangers for directions and the other who wouldn't ask for help even if lost in the Amazon jungle. I'm type 1 – while my cycling friend Sam is type 2. In fact, we're on the extreme ends of the spectrum in this matter.

Sam takes the view that asking others for directions makes one look like an amateur – a wimp. It spoils the adventure, S argues – the fun is in exploration. He refuses to consult online navigation apps. He's like Columbus, looking for India and, sometimes, finding America. But he sticks to his principles. He'd rather wither away and die of thirst than bear the shame of baring his ignorance to strangers.

I am the opposite. I believe that it's only by asking the locals that one can get a leg up on Google Maps, discover hidden gems, and deviate from oft-trodden paths. Above all, I have no sense of direction. I struggle to find my own home. I don't have a compass in my head – or if I do, it desperately needs correction. It has an error of 180 degrees. If you have the misfortune to ask me for directions, do the opposite of my instruction. Turn left if I say turn right. Go north if I recommend south.

I ask anyone who in my estimation has a better sense of direction than me. That is almost everyone. However, I'm rarely misled – I have a strategy. Having been brought up in India, I do the thing that Indians do well. I ask more than one person the same question, discreetly. I then adopt the majority opinion. This works.

Sam was ill last Sunday and I did the ride on my own. I found my own way to Stockbridge, an idyllic little town, population of 592 as per the last census, in rural Hampshire. I had coffee and a croissant in a café situated above a channel of the River Test. I struck up conversation with other customers, patted wet dogs, and discussed routes with cyclists who came in for a cuppa. The warmth of the July sun – the gentle breeze in my hair – and the delighted squeal of children as they ran along the riverbank imbued the atmosphere with a sense of calm and wellbeing. Staring at the flowing water, I slipped into a meditative trance.

After a while, I decided to walk along the path by the channel. Rolling my bike along the bank, and manoeuvring it through narrow stiles, I reached an expansive marshland – a haven for ground-nesting birds, as S had once told me. He is quite an amateur ornithologist and often stops to regale me with interesting facts about the local birds. I missed his company, but was equally happy on my own. There were no other cyclists around, as cycling was not permitted in the area.

Two elderly men were walking towards me with their dogs. I asked the first one,

"Where's the exit from this park, please?"

"I'm not too sure. I live in Winchester. My brother may know," he pointed at his companion, following some twenty metres behind him.

I then asked the other man,

"Hello, your brother says you would know where the exit is."

"It's that way, at the far corner," he pointed. I was a bit

concerned at the steep angle of his pointing arm.

"Couple of miles at least," he warned.

So, I asked another couple walking their black Labrador. They confirmed the brother's direction but asked why I wasn't riding my bike. I said I wasn't allowed to and told them about the ground-nesting birds. After exchanging some pleasantries, I moved on and repeated my question to a young couple who seemed like locals.

"There's a gate right there," the young woman told me. "Go through and you can ride for miles along the old railway track."

I didn't ask anyone else. I broke my 'majority wins' rule because I was confident in her local knowledge. After a few hundred metres of rolling my bike, I was at a gate that led to a little off-road track. For the next five miles or so, I was on National Cycle Route 246 – also known as the Test Way – running along the River Test. There was greenery everywhere, making one momentarily forget there were other colours in nature – such was the preponderance of green. Then suddenly, wild flowers danced in the air like little musical notations as I whooshed past them. Flashes of bright orange, purple and yellow colour. A butterfly raced ahead briefly before disappearing into the wilderness. The river strummed a steady rhythm as it flowed at pace, heading for Southampton Water.

I reached home just in time to catch the Wimbledon finals on TV. By asking people for directions, I discovered the Test Way. Otherwise, I would've taken the dreary road route. I was as excited by my adventure as Enid Blyton's Famous Five were with theirs. Best of all, I didn't get lost that day like I usually do. Perhaps my mental compass is slowly correcting itself.

~

37

Where has that India Gone?

(This was published in 2023 by IndianLink, Australia)

Kerala, my native state: the azan from the local mosque wakes me up. It starts our day. We don't think Muslim or Mosque. It is an alarm clock. Time to get up and do our homework before school.

Women troop to the local temple clutching bunches of wild flowers, their hair still wet from the morning dip in the river. The deities at the local temple receive their floral offering. We don't think Hindu, but wait for them to return home carrying the fragrance of sandalwood and basil. And prepare breakfast – inshallah, steaming idlis and coconut chutney.

On Sunday morning, people in their finery throng the church. The women fold their *mundus*[7] in the shape of a Japanese fan. Their gold ornaments glitter in the tropical sun. We don't think Christian but recognise Sundays from their attire. No school, no homework, just playing cricket and climbing trees.

We are in Delhi. It is midwinter. At 4 a.m. a procession of men and women singing hymns marches through the streets. We don't think Sikhs but know it is the birthday of one of the Gurus. We smile and return to the comfort of our blanket.

---

7 *Mundu, a traditional garment worn in Kerala, wrapped around the waist and extending to the ankles.*

We read about people marching without clothes to a temple in Karnataka. There is a move to ban the practice, the papers tell us, due to the outraged morals of those who do not understand the Digambara, wearing the sky, concept. We did not think Jains but our adolescent minds are titillated nevertheless by the thought of naked bodies. And we are intrigued by the rationale behind not wearing clothes – to prevent the death of insects who could be trapped in them. Perhaps, a seed that germinated eventually to turn me vegetarian.

I have been away for over three decades. Things are different now. Religion has somehow become very important, especially other people's. Our identities are now defined by our gods. It seems nothing else matters. Not the neighbourhood, not the profession, not the linguistic commonality. Just gods, who we can't even see.

What has happened to that India of my youth?

~

38

The Mad Bank

I finally decided to update my mobile number on my bank's system. It had become impossible to conduct even simple transactions. Everything needs verification through OTP – one-time password. OTPs, like oxygen, sustain life. Without them you will wither away. However, unlike oxygen, they will also drive you insane. What else could explain the madness meted out by the bank?

My mobile phone company had recently deactivated my phone number although I was keeping it live by paying the minimum charges every month. The reason for this deactivation was that my passport registered with them had expired and I had not updated their system. No warning – not a sausage. Anyway, as my bank had the deactivated mobile number in its system, I was not receiving any OTPs. I was unable to conduct simple transactions. My own money, like a mirage, had become unreachable. I was withering.

With great trepidation I dived into the depths of my bank's online system. One doesn't need a degree in software engineering to know that no functionality should be hidden away at more than two levels in a menu system. Here I was deep diving into fifth layers and discovering deeper layers indicated by the dreaded three dots. Finally, by sheer luck, I discovered a form that I could use to request a number change. Another form? Here starts my trouble. But I was already beginning to fade away due to the lack of OTPs. My oxygen levels were dangerously low. I downloaded the form.

The mobile number 'updation' – put that new word in your pipe and smoke it, you rigid Victorian Oxford dictionary – form was refreshingly simple. It did not ask for my father's name or my grandmother's notarised birth certificate. No – just my old and new phone numbers. And a self-attested copy of my passport. Simple. At long last, my bank has discovered simplicity and elegance in form design.

Within ten minutes, digital images of the above documents were dispatched to SpecialCustomers@madbank.co.in. A couple of days later, I received a response:

> *Kindly note that the signature mentioned on your mobile number update form does not match with our bank records. Hence we request you to resend the mobile number update request with correct signature along with self-attested scan copy of identity proof.*

So, I did it all over again, and sent it. I then received the exact same message – *'your current signature does not match the existing record.'*

So, I did it all over again; sorry to repeat myself – but I have no better words to express this concisely.

No luck – the bank was adamant. It was a different person who wrote to me each time. But the words were the same.

By this time, I had lost my rag. I knew I was going to die if I couldn't receive OTPs. So, what does a dying man care? I signed the form not once, but ten times and in four different colours – red, blue, green and black.

Fourth time lucky! I received a somewhat positive

response that stated that the mobile "updation" process had started and that if I don't hear from them again, I am on my way to success. It was just so refreshing. I could begin to breathe again.

A day later, I received the following email:

> *We are unable to process your request for change of mobile number due to multiple signatures mentioned on request letter.*
>
> *We request you, to please resend the request letter by mentioning the correct signature in order to accept your request and proceed further.*

By this time, I didn't care, so I picked out the second or third form that was summarily rejected and sent it again. You might think that was a desperately stupid thing to do. But when you realise that reason and logic are not the forte of my bank, you will understand my action. Beat mad logic with madder logic.

To my last application, I received the following response:

> *Your new phone number ending 914 has been successfully updated.*

Now I am drowning in OTPs. Death by drowning, I understand, is more bearable than death by asphyxiation.

~

39

Form-Fill Phobia

This is my last ploy to avoid filling that form. The time I spend writing this will take me close to noon, at which time I have to go somewhere. Maybe I'll return to the form tomorrow.

The bank has been waiting for my input for several weeks – no, I lie – months. I have a new passport. My KYC – Know Your Customer – details require updating. It should take a normal person around ten minutes. That is assuming the form is normal. But it is as abnormal as a form can get.

I am struggling – I just can't do it. "What's the big deal?" you ask. Well, it starts with my name, Gopinath Odayammadath Chandroth. It has 29 letters but the form does not have sufficient boxes. Neither is there any blank space for those with long names. And no shortening is allowed – you must write your name in full and limit it within the number of boxes we provide you because we have designed the form as if it were a paper form although everything is entirely electronic – online. But still we are stuck in the days of paper and we want you to save paper but there is no paper involved.

And if I get it wrong? The form will be rejected. If I move to the next page but want to come back and correct something? Forget it – you cannot do it. We will clear the form for you and you have to do it all over again – it is for your own security! So, I brave the Gods, defy the rules and divide the boxes carefully with a ruler. Now I have converted 20 boxes to 30 (by subdividing the last 10 into 20 half boxes). How ingenious! If you don't give me enough boxes, I shall make my own. This is the beauty of the Indian marine engineer. Resourceful. I write my name in font size 6.

Next row – father's name! Kalliattu Thazhathuveettil Harindranath. Only 37 letters. No problem. I have mastered the technology of box dividing.

Moving on ... Third row: Maiden name. But I don't have a maiden name. I thought long and hard about this problem. Weeks elapsed without result. All information MUST be given in full – the form screamed at me in bold red. What to do? I had run out of ideas. Shall I invent a maiden name? Didn't some famous psychologist declare that we all have a bit of the other gender in us? But if I do make up one, will they ask me for an apostilled document of proof? Has my bank bought the idea of gender fluidity? Na! They can't get away from paper, even when they go paperless. It must be something far more serious.

I decided to call my relationship manager (RM) and ask him. The innocent among you would be thinking, "Why didn't he just call his relationship manager in the first place?" That's because you are not familiar with this ilk of bank employees. If you are not already up the wall, the RM will make sure you get there in quick time. I always use him as a last resort. When I am at my wit's end. The conversation went like this:

"Sir, just fill in your mother's maiden name."

"But it doesn't ask for my mother's maiden name. It is asking for mine."

"Yes sir, but men don't have maiden names!"

"Exactly – then why ask me for this information?"

"Sir, the form doesn't know you are male."

I gave up. I cannot carry out simple transactions. Like booking air tickets. I must have an OTP (one-time password) to complete the process. But I cannot receive an OTP because my phone number has been deactivated by the phone company. Why? Because I have a new passport and they need me to update their system. They too have a form. I dare not look at it.

~

40

The Difficult Type of Honesty

To be honest with others is fairly easy, but to be honest with oneself is hard and painful. Let me narrate something that happened to me the other day.

I volunteer with an organisation to teach English to asylum seekers. Recently, in a one-to-one lesson, I was banging on about comparative adjectives and imperatives when I noticed my student, I'll call her B, was distracted.

"What's the matter B?" I asked.

"There's no food today. I have no money. I am hungry. My daughter also hungry," she replied.

She pointed at the table in the corner of the teaching hall. It was normally well stocked with free supplies from a local supermarket. Anyone who needs food could help themselves. On the day, however, the table was empty.

I was shocked to hear this. It had not occurred to me until then that people seeking shelter in our midst were going hungry. I couldn't give her some money because our organisation doesn't approve of it. Moreover, it would have been humiliating for B to receive such largesse from me. I racked my brain for a solution and soon found it, right under my nose.

B and her daughter could have langar at one of the local Gurudwaras. Langar, for those who are unfamiliar with the concept, is a tradition in which a Gurudwara offers a free meal to anyone who enters it. I suggested the idea to B who requested me to accompany her. We fixed a date and time to test out the langar idea.

On the agreed date, a woman teacher and I met B outside a Gurudwara. Having removed our shoes and covered our heads, we entered. Each of us picked up a thali – a steel tray with little moulded sections that segregate items of food – and were served chapatis, dal and raita. Simple but wholesome food.

We finished eating. The ladies were chatting with some others at our table. I took my plate to the washing-up area. After washing the thali, I rested it on its edge on the draining board and started to make my way back to the dining area. This is when my trouble began. An elderly gentleman with a flowing white beard and red turban called out to me, "Oye, you! Come back here. Where do you think you are going? Who will dry the plates?"

Now, I have forgotten the last time when someone spoke to me in such a peremptory tone. This man was treating me like a wayward brat. I was confused and promptly apologised to him for my omission. Going back to the stack of plates, I picked up a few and dried them. By the time I finished, the man had gone from the room.

When I was back in the dining room, he confronted me again.

"Didn't I tell you to dry the plates?" he scolded me in Hindi, "Go back and dry them." He pointed an imperious finger in the direction of the cleaning area.

By then I was beginning to get a hold of myself. However, not wanting to create a scene, I smiled at him and said firmly in Hindi, "No. I am not going back there. I have done a few.

That's enough."

"You won't do it?" he said, "then you won't get any more food here."

By then the ladies joined me. Thankfully, they were ignorant of the situation. They gushed with praise for the generosity of the Gurudwara and the selfless people who served there. I was distracted and my response was subdued. Although I kept the incident from them, it was playing in an infinite loop in my head as I drove home, like a computer programme with a bug.

I continued to rage internally all evening. I couldn't understand the turmoil in my mind. Why was I feeling so bad? Could I not just forget the incident? Wasn't it the result of just an ignorant man having a bad day? But there was no respite. A gale force wind continued to blow inside me. The question that bothered me the most was – why did it affect me so much? Deep inside, I think I knew the answer. But I refused to accept it and looked for a better, lofty solution to my predicament.

If this man could treat me like this, he must be treating many others the same way. Yes! That's it. I was outraged on behalf of those faceless unfortunates who go there to have one good meal a day. How dare he treat my brothers and sisters so? Time for retribution.

The next morning, I went to an Asian shop and purchased two small sacks of wheat flour. Then I drove to the Gurudwara and was directed to take my contribution to the kitchen. By donating the flour, I had established that I was not a freeloader. By abandoning my waxed jacket for a conventional one, I had rid myself of the shabby – posh to the discerning

– look. Back in the dining hall, I met the same old man. He looked a bit peeved and after the customary 'Sat Sri Akal', I confronted him.

"You shouted at me yesterday. Do you treat everyone the same way? Doesn't it go against everything that the Gurudwara stands for? Respect and dignity for all? Universal brotherhood?" I lectured him. His colleagues were beginning to gather around us.

"I am sorry," said the old man, "the thing is so many people come here and leave their plates dirty..."

"Yes, that's precisely the point. You can tell them nicely. There is a way to talk...*baat karne ka tareeka hota hai...*" and so on and so forth, I continued to harangue him. One by one, all of them apologised to me. They invited me to have some langar, get some *prasad*. I went up to where the Granth Sahib was being worshipped, took some prasad and left the place. I felt vindicated. I had won.

My victory was, however, short-lived. The storm in my mind continued to rage. I couldn't escape the real question:

Am I affronted on behalf of all the others insulted by this man? Or is it just the personal humiliation that hurt me more? The alternatives were inseparable, like a mental vichyssoise.

I stewed in confusion for a couple of days and then decided to call a close friend back in India. He was my classmate. As twenty year old engineering students, we used to roam the streets of Calcutta every evening discussing among other things, the delusional nature of human thoughts.

After telling him the whole story, I asked him, "So why do I feel hurt? Is it because my pride was hurt? Or is it because I was concerned about all those others who may have suffered at his hands?"

"It is your pride, your ego," he said simply.

He was not the type to mince his words and went on to present his thoughts. It was a clear, painfully trenchant analysis of the episode. He didn't say anything new and only confirmed what I knew deep inside but was not honest enough to dredge up. The mental soup was beginning to separate into its elements.

My ego had taken a severe beating because a stranger had managed to see a different me. There I was, in my eyes: a respectable member of society, educated, well read, well dressed in a posh Barbour waxed jacket, gainfully employed for over forty years. And there I was, in another man's perspective: a scrounger looking for a free meal, down and out, poverty stricken, a rough sleeping vagabond – 'just look at his coat' – taking advantage of the Gurudwara's generosity.

I don't like this other persona he saw. I can't bear to think what that says about me. So, I will keep that analysis for another day. Yes, the thought did occur to me that the man must have been treating others with similar disrespect. But that was only a weak corollary – an also-ran. In all honesty, it was all about me!

~

41

Where Are You (Really) From?

"Where are you from?" enquired the 83-year-old *lady-in-waiting* of a black woman at a charity event at the palace. Henceforth, I'll call the *lady-in-waiting,* Lady W.

"Hackney," replied the woman.

Not receiving the answer she wanted, Lady W persisted,

"No, but where are you really from?"

This line of questioning continued in an unusually offensive manner. Eventually, the hapless woman at the receiving end finished the conversation thus:

"No, Lady. I am of African heritage, Caribbean descent and British nationality."

The media got hold of the story. Lady W was subsequently sacked for this overt act of racism and the palace apologised profusely to the victim. It's an old story – but what's it got to do with me?

Occasionally, I too get asked where I am from. A typical conversation is as follows: "So, Gopi, where are you from?"

"Southampton," I reply while observing the other person's facial expression to gauge if my response was satisfactory. Often, I spot a fleeting look of disappointment on my interlocutor's face. In this case, I quickly add, "I am originally from India. I have lived in this country since 1992." I have this habit of supplying more information than solicited, but I find it sometimes leads to interesting conversations.

"India?" he says, "Fascinating place. I was there on vacation last year..." and the conversation takes off. I am hanging on their every word, wallowing in nostalgia for my home country while they relive their magical holiday. Everyone's happy. The question, "where are you from?" is, more often than not, an opening gambit to start a conversation. In the vast majority of instances, no racism is intended, and none taken.

Let me illustrate a couple of anecdotes.

I visited Tripoli, Libya, in the early years of my sailing career. After calling at Aden, my first foreign port and then capital of Yemen, and transiting the Suez Canal, my ship called at Tripoli. Libya was a wealthy nation at the time. It was a decade before the Lockerbie bombing and subsequent sanctions that eviscerated the country's economy.

One evening, I was wandering aimlessly in Tripoli taking in the sights of its palm-lined avenues, the din and smells of its souks. Near the main square, I spotted a middle-aged man leaning against a flashy sports car, enjoying a cigarette. He looked like the carbon copy of my favourite uncle back home. The sight of this man simultaneously made me homesick and raised my spirits. Approaching him, I asked, "Are you from India?"

The uncle-lookalike gave me a long hard stare and replied, "And if I am not, what will you do to me?"

I apologised profusely and explained why I had assumed he was from India. He was only half impressed with my grovelling. With the special trait of people from the subcontinent – of ticking someone off while also giving them advice – he said, "I am from Pakistan. Never ask anyone such a question in the future."

Thank you, my Pakistani uncle, for this life lesson, and for the coffee and cake you subsequently bought me. I was a wiser 22-year-old after that incident and always took special care while attempting to establish someone's country of origin. The habit of trying to understand where someone is 'really' from, their human provenance – so to speak, never left me.

Some fifteen years later, I decided to hang up my sea boots and settle ashore. I ended up working for the University of Sheffield in its Computer Science department. A colleague with a very distinct guttural accent used to work in an adjoining office. He didn't sound anything like the locals and rarely smiled or acknowledged my presence. I was only coming to grips with the strong 'owts' and 'nowts' of the broad Yorkshire accent. My curiosity to establish his ethnicity egged me on. After some heavy digging, I concluded that he could be Scottish. I had never come across a Scotsman until then. Keen to validate my tentative conclusion, I asked, "Is that a Scottish accent?"

"How did ya guess?" he replied, half growling, half smiling, in what I know today to be the Glaswegian accent.

On that occasion, however, his sarcasm was lost on me. Nevertheless, we became good friends. He regaled me with extraordinary tales about the Loch Ness monster, the Highlands and the Lowlands, and nuances of single malt whiskies from these lands. "Oh aye – it's the water," he'd say. I found myself working in Glasgow some ten years later, thanks perhaps to my obsessive curiosity that led to a fruitful friendship with a Glaswegian.

And finally I retired in 2022. On a balmy summer morning, I was cycling with a group of about fifteen others on a local club ride in Southampton. When we reached a quiet stretch of road in Hampshire, someone rode up and cycled alongside me. After mutual introductions, he asked, "So, where do you come from?"

"India," I replied, assuming he wanted to have a conversation with me about India and so jumping straight to the right answer. Except it was the wrong answer. He chuckled. "It's a long way to cycle!" he said, "I meant where did you start from this morning?"

So, in conclusion, establishing someone's origin is fraught with danger. It can go wrong in many ways if one is not careful. Human communication is imperfect and often words only convey a fraction of what we want to say. It is easy enough to misconstrue the language of others.

This is not condoning the brazenly racist approach of Lady W – her line of questioning was completely out of order. But she was the exception – a rotten apple in an otherwise good basket.

~

42

Oh Lebanon!

"Captain – for God's sake – always go ashore in groups of five or more."

The ship's agent had just come aboard in Tripoli, Lebanon, and was not wasting time on pleasantries. He mimed a pistol to his temple.

"You could be shot if you walk around on your own."

That was my welcome to Lebanon in the early 1990s. I remembered something my eldest brother once told me: "One who generalises, generally lies."

As I travelled the world for fifteen years as a young marine engineer, this aphorism had repeatedly proven true. Yet here I was, in Tripoli, weighing the agent's dramatic warning against my instinct to explore.

My mental calculus ran like this: Perhaps there had been a stray incident or two during the civil war, which had officially ended only a few years earlier. The agent had likely extrapolated those into blanket caution. That couldn't be right. I would take my chances.

While working on ships, I generally went ashore alone. It wasn't that I disliked company – but I was a poor match for the carousal and chaos of the typical sailor on shore leave. I preferred to explore, observe, and soak in the spirit of a place. My usual routine went like this:

- Find a taxi driver with some English.
- Agree on a two-hour tour without bargaining.
- Ask them to show me the city's highest point, a rich neighbourhood, a poor one, a significant place of worship, and any site of local interest.

It was a system that rarely failed me.

As I scanned the port for a likely driver, a man approached. He put his hand in his trouser pocket and began to withdraw something. I braced myself, sure my end was imminent. But he pulled out a cigarette instead, lit it, and gave me a long, neutral look. No gun, no danger. Just a moment of unnecessary panic. I laughed at myself inwardly.

Soon I found a driver. Over the next couple of hours, I absorbed Tripoli: its ancient citadel, the labyrinthine souks, its skyline pierced by minarets. Later, walking alone through quieter streets, I came across a row of old railway carriages – some burnt, some intact. Families lived in them. I approached carefully, without intruding.

The women had the kind of striking beauty that seems carved from sea and stone – eyes the colour of Mediterranean mist. Their children, barefoot and shrieking with laughter, darted between the iron wheels of their homes. They wore rags but radiated joy. The image is still etched on my mind – a symbol of a journey stalled by war, and a people quietly preparing to move again.

As the sun began to set, the muezzin's call to prayer softened the air. I wandered into a small café where older men smoked hookahs and played cards. Though I understood no Arabic, the smiles were broad and the hand-to-heart gestures warm. I ordered a hookah and some coffee. Unrequested plates of food appeared.

Someone brought out a chessboard. We played a couple of games. Strangers gathered to advise on strategy, laughing and arguing in equal measure. I was no longer a foreigner – just another player at the table. When I rose to leave and offered to pay, the café owner refused.

"No, no, friend. No money," he said, placing a hand on his chest.

He returned with his battered old car, gestured for me to get in, and drove me back to the ship. We passed the train carriages again, now faintly lit, smoke curling from makeshift chimneys. I imagined the women preparing supper under starlight. The night sky was bright and still – like a protective dome over everything below.

I felt safe. There was no sniper. No threat. Just a man giving another man a lift home.

That's the thing about assumptions – they're always too small for the people we apply them to.

~

43

Salsa Sally

My salsa instructor Sally,
Brims with style and grace.
She flexes and twists, like a mystical snake,
And flows like a river in spate.
Struggling to follow her gyrations,
I'm decrepit with wear and tear,
I move like a block of wood,
I'm a pathetic shuffling bear.
So what? a voice consoles,
You're educated, even bright.
You may be clumsy, a dancer sans clue,
But you have brains, you're erudite.
And she? the voice continues,
She's graceful, but no scholarly flair.
She may be a danseuse lithe,
But all performance, not much upstairs.
And then one day I saw her name,
Headlined in the morning paper,
Dr Sally Hasburg, professor of physics,
Prize-winning salsa dancer.

~

44

A Young Man in an Old Person's Skin

One of the guiding principles of my life comes from Max Ehrmann's Desiderata, a prose poem I've turned to many times. Among other things, it says:

'Take kindly the counsel of the years, gracefully surrendering the things of youth.'

A recent brush with bank fraud reminded me how hard that is to do.

Last week, I received two envelopes from Barclays Bank. One contained a debit card and the other a PIN number.

"Dear Dr Chandroth," said the letter, "You're ready to go online ... All you need to do now is sit back and enjoy an easy way to bank online."

What's the catch? I never opened an account with Barclays. Never banked with them. Never planned to.

I called the bank. It was late evening on Saturday. The recorded message said I should call back during weekdays – unless I was reporting fraud.

A young-sounding woman with an Indian accent picked up.

"I apologise for the inconvenience, Dr Chandroth," she said, following the usual script.

She then proceeded to record all my personal details, including date and place of birth, and finally assured me that the fake account would be blocked. I needn't worry anymore.

Then she asked if there was anything else she could help with.

"How is it possible for someone to open an account in my name? Don't you verify their bona fides?" I asked calmly.

"Dr Chandroth, fraudsters target vulnerable and elderly people," she replied, quite casually.

Now, I should have remained calm. But truth be told – I was livid. "Elderly?" "Vulnerable?" Me?!

I'd never thought of myself in those terms. But when someone catches you off guard, the reaction reveals a lot. Her words struck a couple of raw nerves.

"I am not vulnerable. I have a PhD in Computer Science. I cycled 70 kilometres just last week. How many kilometres can you do? I am not some doddering old geezer. What is vulnerable is your bank's security, not me!" I ranted.

"I am so sorry, sir. I didn't mean you are old and vulnerable. Age is just a number," the poor woman replied, distraught and clearly off-script.

I too am sorry, young lady, for my intemperate outburst. I am probably three times your age. Of course, you consider me elderly and, by definition, vulnerable. I promise to improve and – to 'take kindly the counsel of the years.' But I'll be damned if I surrender the things of youth.

Now, where's my OAP travel pass? I'm ditching the bike today. A nice calming bus ride should soothe my 'elderly nerves.'

~

45

Truth, Lies and Half-Truths

Mahatma Gandhi once said, *The truth must manifest in your thoughts, your words and your actions.* I've reflected on this often – it's a lofty ideal, no doubt. But I try – not always successfully. The only saving grace is that I catch myself when I stray from this principle. "Don't do it again," I chastise my lying self and promise to do better.

The following is an undiluted true story.

The other day, I was on a bike ride with my cycling buddy – let's call him Sam. We were on a country road with barely any traffic. It was a warm autumn afternoon, a tailwind helped us, and everything was fine with the world. Leaves on trees were beginning to turn a shade yellow. They trembled in the breeze as if with a foreboding of imminent demise.

"What's one thing that you are proud of?" Sam asked me, completely out of the blue.

I replied without hesitation, "I like to think I tell the truth 99% of the time," I said, without missing a beat.

"Really?"

"Really," I replied with conviction.

"Wow!" he said and was quiet for a couple of miles. I could sense he was impressed and was giving it some deep churn.

"Ok. Tell me, what's one thing you are not proud of?"

"Whenever I hear something good has happened to

someone – other than immediate family and a few close friends – my first reaction (for milliseconds only, is envy," I declared, stressing the qualifier just in case he got the wrong idea.

"Good God! That's not good G. Not good at all. You must do better."

"I know. I have been trying," I responded as we entered a built-up area.

Cycling has this curious effect on people. As the scenery around one changes, the conversation changes to suit. Spotting a German-registered car ahead, I reminisced about my recent holidays in Berlin and Amsterdam.

"Oh by the way, I will be in India most of December," I informed him.

"You must be well-off to afford all these trips," Sam said. "Do you have a decent pension?"

"I'm OK," I confessed.

"You know," he said, "I had a G moment there. Briefly, I was quite jealous!"

I gloated. Finally, a small win for Team Honesty.

How was I to know then that Sam would have the last laugh on the Truth principle? All the same, I appreciated his candour. We parted company with plans to meet the following Sunday.

The next day, I booked two tickets for a play at the theatre near my house. The play was on a Thursday at 7:30 p.m. Somehow, I had forgotten the date but 'Thursday' had stuck in my mind. On 13 October, also a Thursday, my wife and I went to attend a meeting in Southampton. The meeting was scheduled for 7:30 p.m. At 7:25, panic set in.

"We forgot the play!" I exclaimed – heavy with the unspoken implication that this was her fault, not mine. My wife didn't remember the details either but let me do the panicking while she concentrated even harder on her Sudoku puzzle.

Quite fortuitously, I remembered I had paid a couple of pounds while booking the tickets as an insurance in case I couldn't attend.

I had five minutes to deal with the situation because once I crossed the 7:30 mark, I wouldn't have been able to claim a refund. At lightning speed, I wrote to the theatre:

"Due to personal reasons, I am unable to attend this evening's show. Kindly issue a refund."

I had considered saying I had fallen ill. But that would be a blatant lie, so I decided against it. 'Personal reasons' could be anything, including having senior moments bordering on early onset of dementia. I knew I was dancing on the head of a pin here – perhaps in a court of law I might have scraped through. But in the court of my conscience, I was already guilty.

The next day, 14 October, I received a response from the theatre:

"You are booked for Thursday, 27 October. You haven't missed it!"

I was glad I didn't lose any money. However, I realised I had overestimated myself in the Truth department. In an email to Sam, I narrated the mix-up with the theatre tickets, concluding:

I want you to delete what I said about me being truthful 99% of the time...

Very disappointed in myself. Must try harder.

Maybe settle for 95%?

See you Sunday.

G

~

46

Sherlock Holmes Near Home

Last night I attended my first performance by the Chameleon Theatre Company – just a ten-minute walk from my house in Chandler's Ford. Despite living here for twelve years, I'd never stepped inside the venue until a tip from Janet, editor of website ChandlersFordToday, pointed me there. The production, *Sherlock Holmes and the Mystery at Mallen Hall,* proved a revelation – and made me reflect on the old Malayalam saying: 'The jasmine in one's own garden has no fragrance,' a proverb reminding us that we often overlook the treasures in our own backyard.

The tickets were reasonably priced and the show played to a full house. The acoustics were impressive – dialogues came across crisp and clear even to those of us who sat in the back rows. In my youth, I read several Sherlock Holmes mysteries, but this was the first time I watched a live enactment. What a performance it was! Holmes, Dr Watson, and the other characters acted with grace and élan.

Very quickly, I forgot I was watching actors in a scripted play. I felt like a fly on the wall in the elegantly set stage of a late nineteenth-century living room. My immersion in the play was total.

During the interval, the audience enjoyed glasses of wine and light refreshments at prices less than a quarter of those charged by London theatres.

In the second half, Sherlock and Watson tackled the

murder of Sir Howard Latham and the mysterious death of his dog a week prior. Plots and sub-plots, intrigues and rabbit holes – Holmes, assisted by Dr Watson, untangled the knots with delightful craftsmanship. They employed a methodical process of elimination, observation of known facts, and inference. "Elementary, Mr Watson," Holmes interjected occasionally in his inimitable style.

Then, without warning, a picture on the wall fell down! It took the actors by surprise and tickled the audience. This unplanned incident somehow made the occasion even more special. I could sense the bonhomie in the room: the mirth of the audience melding with the amusement of the actors, imbuing a sense of uniqueness. The incident was soon forgotten and the detectives continued their quest, magnifying glass and all.

Sherlock Holmes then came up with the idea of reconstructing the scene of the crime. He asked Emily Latham and her brother Roger Latham for details of the room where their father's body was found.

"There was a writing table here," said Emily, and Dr Watson moved a desk accordingly. The chairs were rearranged closer to the fireplace, and the doors at either end of the stage were demarcated – one leading to the garden, the other to the front lobby.

Then Sherlock, strictly following the script, asked, "Were there any pictures on the wall?"

The audience burst into laughter. I assumed the timing was a deliberate comic touch, but later discovered it was, in fact, part of the script.

"Not anymore!" someone quipped, while others chimed in with witty remarks. Even the actors struggled to suppress their amusement. It was a moment I will not forget. Considering Christmas is around the corner, I wondered aloud to my wife if this was part pantomime.

Emily Latham finally gave us the stern look of a schoolteacher and, with an endearing smile, told us to shush.

The play continued. The mystery was finally solved and the murderer arrested. We clapped until our hands hurt. For a modest local theatre, it delivered a thoroughly memorable evening – clever, warm-hearted, and full of character.

~

47

Video Bell

Are you a good liar? If not, don't buy a video doorbell. Now, why do I say this? I always analyse the risks of actions I intend to take. So, when someone suggested I purchase a video doorbell, my first thought was: 'That's a great idea.' However, when I started analysing future scenarios, I wasn't too sure.

Mr Thief rings the bell. I am not home. In fact, I am abroad.

"I have a parcel for you."

"Ah! Please leave it with the neighbour."

"Why don't you open the door and take it?"

"I am not home."

"I see. Maybe I can return tomorrow with the parcel?"

"No. I won't be back tomorrow."

The thief is now licking his lips, hatching a plan. Time is his ally. He is looking around, gauging the doors, scanning for cameras, generally taking stock. He is momentarily distracted.

"When will you be back?"

"Two weeks Monday."

"OK. Cool."

Cool, indeed.

Some of you must be wondering why I am giving away all the information to a stranger. The thing is, I don't know what else to do. I find it hard to lie. Not because I am the paragon of Truth, but because I always get caught when I lie. So, for a long, long time now, I haven't lied to anyone.

I'm also too generous with information. If I don't tell you every last detail, I somehow feel I am being devious – disingenuous.

Consider the same scenario with an alternative dialogue.

Ring-ring. Mr Thief, carrying a package, is at my door.

"I have a parcel for you."

"Please leave it with the neighbour."

"Why don't you take it yourself?"

"I'm in the shower."

"I'll wait."

"No... Please leave it with the neighbour."

"Where are you?"

"In the shower."

"Yes, but are you in your own shower or somewhere else?"

"Hmm... aaah... I'm not home."

"OK. I can come back tomorrow."

"No..."

"So, you're not back tomorrow?"

"Hmmm... aaahh... No. I'm abroad. Back in two weeks."

"Cool."

I am, therefore, still considering if I should install a video doorbell. Will it convert me – an honest, straightforward, naïve man – into a devious, lying crook?

~

48

Burglary

My car, bicycle and a few other things were stolen on 6 August, Saturday. It has been a traumatic few days. I am dealing with the insurance, police, locksmiths, security alarm vendors, and others. Money is haemorrhaging. Mental health has dropped from 9/10 to 3/10.

On Saturday morning, the police visited me and spent a few hours writing my statement and managing my expectations. When they finished, the young police officer told me, "We also need to write another report on how you feel."

I was too polite to tell her, "That report needn't be very long. It starts with an F and ends with a D."

The car was found on Monday, abandoned a couple of miles away from my house. I have consented to the police carrying out a forensic examination on it. I am told it is undamaged.

It is an old car – 15 years old, to be precise. I had not realised it until it was stolen – I was very attached to the car. It was like losing a dog who came to us as a pup and grew old with us. It is curious how one attributes sentience to inanimate objects. Anthropomorphism is the word, I believe.

I remember the following thoughts going through my mind:

I hope the car is not being used to commit crimes

I hope they don't burn it

I hope they don't ram it against something

I did worry about the huge amount of money that I would have to fork out to replace the car. However, that was not the predominant thought that occupied my mind.

When my dog Monty died, people asked me if I would replace him.

"Monty is irreplaceable," was my standard response. I feel the same about my car.

~

49

The Planet and Me

The other day, on BBC Radio 4, I heard an interview with the founder of a car-free-society campaign. When she was asked if she owned a car, she sheepishly admitted,

"Yes I do, because ..."

I am like her in many ways when it comes to my environmental credentials. I too have a 'because', in fact several. I am not an eco-warrior but want to do my bit for the planet.

I ask myself:

Do I really care about the planet?

Answer: Yes, very much.

Am I doing all the right things?

Answer: Yes and no.

I am certainly not a Trumpian climate-change denier. I am acutely aware that our planet, like a slowly flooding ship, is fast approaching its endgame. Unlike the crew on a sinking ship working with single-minded focus to stop the flooding, I just live my life without panic. Perhaps I believe the climate crisis is not imminent, because it will not affect me tomorrow or next month or next year. I don't behave with the sense of urgency of the crew of the sinking ship. Just the same, I know fully well that I am in a slow-motion car crash. But I just carry on, arranging the deck chairs on the Titanic, as they say. So, why don't I act?

The astronomers predict that the sun will go out in 7–8 billion years. Most of us don't worry about it. However, the Earth crisis is happening all around us. Forest fires, record-breaking temperatures, floods, rising sea levels ... we know all this. Some of us physically experience these. Yet it is not as urgent as the sinking ship. It is not happening to me as I write this. One could argue that the turmoil around the world today is a consequence of global warming. However, that argument is tenuous and open to endless debate. The planet crisis is not in our face – and there is the crunch.

Let us consider what we could do. On an individual basis, the things we can do are limited. It is unrealistic to expect the general public to turn into eco-warriors overnight. We do what we can and what we must. Incandescent bulbs are not available to purchase, so we buy LED bulbs. It saves us money in electricity bills and saves the environment. I think our (governments') quest must fit this model. Only then will our collective endeavour succeed.

Let me list what I, personally, do and don't do:

I segregate my garbage, take the bottles to the bottle bank, and I carry my own bags to the shops. I suffer a twinge of guilt when I buy fruits and vegetables flown across the world and avoid them if there is a home-grown alternative. I have installed solar photovoltaic panels and a water heater on my roof. I am a semi-vegan vegetarian, but that's only because of my personal beliefs about the morality of killing or exploiting animals for my taste.

I take flights as and when required without thinking about the heavy carbon footprint of my journeys. I recently bought a diesel car for my son in spite of its polluting potential. I look at the price tag first and the environment next. Not the other way round.

Without wanting to be too presumptuous, but based on my observation of people I interact with, my guess is a lot of people are like me. Doing what we can, as long as it does not curb our lifestyle too much or significantly dent our bank balance.

Why don't I do more? The honest answer is I don't know what else I could do. As soon as I start looking deeper into environmentally friendly solutions, e.g. swapping to an electric car, I run into several counter arguments. The cobalt mines in Congo and the exploitative nature of its extraction (cobalt is used in batteries), the polluting power plants that produce the electricity to charge my car. But most importantly, the serious price differential between a hydrocarbon fuel-powered car and an electric car. I care more about my wallet than the environment.

I end this with an open question: How do you deal with this issue?

~

50

The Talking Robot

There are two types of people: the types who are polite to Alexa, Siri and similar others, and my type who treat them with mild contempt. My wife and I have this ongoing debate along the lines of, "It's only a machine. Why waste your breath?"

"You can still be polite. What do you lose?"

We have not resolved this argument.

For example, my wife goes, "Alexa, please switch on the light; Alexa, tell me what's fata morgana, please; Alexa, thank-yous very much."

My interaction is similar, but I miss out the pleases and thank you's.

I have a reason.

Way back in 1997, I was a PhD student and research assistant at the Department of Computer Science, University of Sheffield (DCS). Our group had several students working in robotics and we even had a fully fledged robot, Murphy. Other groups worked in speech recognition and natural language processing (NLP). I used to follow their research with keen interest. Making a computer respond to and understand spoken language is extremely hard – like trying to put toothpaste back in its tube, the pundits said at the time. Alexa and others have come a long way since then, as we know.

One Saturday morning, I took my family to a science fair at Doncaster, a nearby town. There was this robot installed in one of the stalls, with an all-swivelling head and blinking eyes and flashing lights. Its info sheet claimed the robot was able to talk and respond to you just as if it were another human being. I was impressed. 'What's all the fuss at DCS then?' I wondered. Here's a robot which claims to pass the Turing Test – when, judging by its response in a conversation, you can't make out if it's a machine or human.

There was a sign pinned on the robot: 'Talk to me.' That was my cue to put it to a rigorous test. Let me say my academic curiosity got the better of me before you say, "How naïve!"

The conversation with the robot went like this:

"Hello, good morning."

"Good morning, sir. I am Mary, what's your name?"

"I'm Gopi."

"Are you enjoying the day?"

"Oh yes. Very much. Particularly impressed by your NLP abilities."

"N.L. what? Hmm, thank you very much, Gopi."

We had an intelligent conversation touching on politics, the problems of the world and how to solve them, the weather and everything else.

To say I was impressed would not begin to express the amazement and admiration I felt for Mary's creators who had cracked the NLP problem completely. Here was a full-blown, almost sentient, robot who could understand spoken language and speak just like any other human being. How could this be while my colleagues at DCS struggled with rudimentary phrases?

Then I had an idea. My family, including my eight-year-old boy, had moved on to other stalls, bored with my protracted interaction with Mary. Out of the blue, I told Mary, "Fuck off."

Now, I am not a vulgar man. I rarely use four-letter words unless I am in the company of close friends. This was an academic exercise. I wanted to know how Mary, the sentient machine, would react.

A young woman in her late twenties tore out from behind the curtain. Her otherwise pretty face was contorted with anger. She was holding a microphone with a long cable attached to Mary.

"You ... you ... you told me to ..." she stuttered – half sob, half shout.

She would have hit me had my expression not been a mixture of disbelief, shock and disappointment.

My disdain for machines who pretend to understand human language stems from that day at the science fair. I refuse to say 'please' and 'thank you' to Alexa and her ilk.

~

51

Cheap Elephants

I became a member of Costco this week. I was swayed by the owner of a bicycle shop where I had taken my bike for a bit of TLC. For those not familiar with Costco, it is a large store where you pay an annual membership fee for the privilege of shopping there. If you don't know what TLC is, don't worry. I too used to think it's a sandwich. It's not. It's a well-known abbreviation for 'tender loving care'. I don't know where I was when TLC became common parlance. Sorry, I digress.

At the cycle shop, we were talking about the high inflation and cost of living going through the ceiling. "Join Costco," counselled the anorak at the cycle shop. "Things are top-quality and really cheap. Fuel is 20p cheaper!"

I fell for it – hook, line and sinker. This is the problem. When someone comes across as an expert in one field, you tend to think they are equally knowledgeable in all fields – an omniscient demigod of sorts. I didn't waste much time. Within a few hours of returning home, I was a full-blown member of Costco.

We had completed our weekly grocery shopping a day earlier. My car had a full tank of petrol. There was nothing that we really needed. However, I couldn't wait. I had to go and buy all that cheap, high quality stuff.

We visited Costco the day after I got my membership. Yes, the cycle guru was right. Things were cheaper than in high-street stores. However, a vital piece of information was missing in his introduction. I found this out once I was inside the store. As an ex accident investigator, I should have detected the 'non-barking' dog in this situation. But sadly, I didn't.

The size of Costco's shopping trolley should have given me a hint. It was nearly my height. I felt like a child taking a regular supermarket trolley for a spin while his parents were distracted. An entire family could sit in the Costco trolley, if they so wished. I finally reached the shopping aisles and eyeballed the goods on sale. Only then did realisation hit me.

Everything was sold in bulk. You want washing-up liquid? Have 12 litres. You want kitchen towels? Take 96. Beer? Pack of 48, nothing less!

Did this discovery dissuade me? Did I wise up and abort my mission? Nooo! The allure of cheap goods was too powerful. I was soon performing quick mental arithmetic on the cost of products. I was in Ali Baba's cave of bargains. My trolley soon filled up with things until I disappeared behind them. I walked back to my car after paying an eye-watering bill, with loo rolls to last me a lifetime and bequeath some to the next generation, sufficient washing-up liquid to clean the grime of Grimsby, lager to fill a bathtub ...

I hadn't even considered the storage space requirement. The attic is a possibility. So, instead of going to the supermarket, I will be going up to the attic for the next few months, perhaps years?

I have decided to be more discerning of other people's views in the future. It's true what they say about keeping your mind too open. People tend to dump their rubbish into it. What's done is done. I doubt if I'll be visiting Costco any more. False economy, is my verdict. To be fair though, petrol was 7p cheaper.

How true is the wise Indian saying, 'Just because elephants are cheap you don't have to buy them.'

~

52

A Tribute on Father's Day

My dear father,

You died 30 years ago. Who knows where death takes us? Suspending disbelief on matters of the afterlife, let me say thanks to you on Father's Day on the off-chance that somewhere lurks the spirit of our loved ones.

You taught me how to see the funny side of life, how to remain honest despite temptations to be otherwise. By your decent living you showed me how easy it is to be decent.

But above all, you taught me the art of storytelling: how to narrate a tale with a terrific punchline, how to keep the audience guessing and curious about the potential outcome.

Although you lacked the thrift that you tried to inculcate in me, you did warn me about the potential consequences of the profligacy of my youth. You told me that if I didn't think of my financial future, I would end up with nothing but a load of empty boxes in my old age.

For years you made me write a one-third précis of the daily newspaper editorial and corrected my language despite your busy schedule. You inculcated in me the pleasure of reading, the passion for literature. You bribed me with 100 rupees to read Mahatma Gandhi's autobiography when I was just fourteen!

So thanks for everything. I couldn't have asked for more.

~

53

Woof

More than a year has passed since my last long cycle ride. One Sunday, I completed a 34-mile ride with our local cycling club. At the halfway point, we stopped for coffee. Most people in our group purchased cakes, but I, determined not to break my recent anti-sugar resolve, bought a bag of mixed nuts.

Wistfully, I watched Victoria sponges, coffee-walnut pastries, and every other delightful cake vanish into hungry cyclists' mouths. I then noticed that every table had a jar of tiny biscuits. What a nice gesture! One teeny-weeny biscuit couldn't hurt, I thought, as I opened the airtight jar and picked out a heart-shaped one.

As I was about to pop it into my mouth, I saw the word engraved on the biscuit: *Woof.*

~

54

This Miserable Business Called Truth

We are quick to blame others for lying, but rarely do we introspect – do we always speak the truth? Do we have the moral authority to cast that first stone?

Without attempting to pontificate on what the ultimate truth is, let me share my thoughts on this business of truth. Considering MPs will vote today on an issue of conscience and decide whether to remove the UK's prime minister from office, this question is timely.

'The truth must manifest in your thoughts, your words and your actions,' Mahatma Gandhi once said. Put simply, your actions, words and thoughts must not contradict each other. While it is easy to align words and actions, and demonstrate them to be so, how are you going to show that your thoughts were on the same track too? It is impossible – no one can know what you are thinking.

In the case of Boris, and in particular the recent scandals, why did we have to spend millions on enquiries to determine if the PM was lying? Should we really be dancing on the head of a pin to understand what the truth is? Should the truth not be obvious, like the sun in the sky? Shouldn't we just believe the PM and trust what he says?

Ah – trust. That is the key. There are no nuances to truth. There are no shades of truth and untruth. It is binary. A statement that contains even one per cent lie and ninety-nine per cent truth becomes a lie – and that is enough to make us lose trust.

If we had trusted Boris, we wouldn't have suffered all this ball-ache. We would have just said, "The PM says so – so it must be true." However, we didn't. Why? Because he has a history of mixing little lies with big truths and big lies with small truths. From the '£350 million every day to the NHS if only we had Brexit' to the 'ambushed by a cake' drama, we have all been fed adulterated truth. We've lost trust. We don't know what the PM is thinking.

So, MPs, align your thoughts, your words and your actions – do the right thing. Show us your thinking.

~

55

A Glass to the Past

A man on the train asked her, "Are you from Lebanon?"

She stared at him, annoyed that he should accost a strange woman in this way. His large brown eyes held a certain childlike innocence. She didn't have the heart to rebuff him.

"Why Lebanon? I'm from London, by the way," she replied with a half-smile.

"Oh, sorry!" he apologised. "The most beautiful women in the world are from Lebanon."

Years later, they raised their glasses to each other, reminiscing about their first meeting some fifty years ago.

~

56

Photo Feast

Sitting by the canal, I see boats full of tourists glide by. I watch them as if watching my thoughts. Barely conscious of either – boats or thoughts – I slip into a semi-dream of silence and peace.

Then I notice the tourists in a boat point their camera at me. I'm both flattered and surprised. Sooo many photos of me being taken from passing boats. I've never been so pleased. My ego is up there frolicking with clouds.

I get up and start walking. There's a spring in my step, a favourite tune playing on my lips.

That is when I see it: on the building right behind where I was sitting, a marble sculpture of an angel with golden wings and a blue-gold shield – slaying some poor dragon with a golden spear.

~

57

Love – 2050

Anita, in the far corner, has film star looks, Einstein brains. A walking Wikipedia, she's gregarious, always smiling, kind. I melt when she looks my way; her hazel eyes caress me. She doesn't know it, but I love her. Today, I will bare my heart.

It's 6 p.m. The office is nearly empty. My angel is slumped in her chair, arms hanging loose, head flopped down. I start to panic.

"Anita," I call softly, approaching her.

She is motionless, silky hair flutters in the air-con's breeze. I touch her shoulder. An LED display lights up on her forehead. Anita01X17 Error404.

~

58

Eyes That Don't See

When we were in primary school, we read stories in Malayalam, each one invariably ending with a strong moral lesson. It was as if the only purpose of a story was to teach you something worthwhile. If it didn't, it had no business in a textbook. They were probably right, considering the purpose of school is to impart lessons. There must be a place for pointless stories too – something that doesn't harangue you, a tale sufficient in itself just for the telling.

I will concede that in the long run, these lofty stories help you navigate life and survive reasonably unscathed. The proviso is of course that you understand the lesson.

Often one remembers the moral and forgets the story. Something that has remained with me is the adage, 'It's not enough to have eyes, one must also see.'

My phone was running out of juice. Fortunately, my charger was in my cabin bag. However, every charging station in the airport terminal was full. People were queuing with their phones for a bit of charge. They might as well be queuing for drinking water, if you go by the expression on their faces – parched, desperate. Some people were sprawled on the floor, having plugged their devices into low wall sockets.

I too was desperate, as I couldn't contemplate being without my phone until I reached my destination. Eventually, I found a free plug point and headed straight for it. It was at the other end of the terminal. But that was okay as I had all the time in the world.

Having managed to achieve 80% charge on my phone, I triumphantly returned to my seat. My wife was beginning to get impatient and asked me where I had gone. When I told her about the elusive charging points and my successful mission to find a free plug point, she pointed to a plug point tucked away between my seat and the adjacent one.

The moral of this story? Yes, of course – if you have eyes, you must also see. But the stronger moral, I think, is this: look under your nose before you search in the neighbour's house.

~

59

The Cure for Boredom

'When you have nothing better to do, write a story': an old iPog saying.

I am stuck in the departure lounge of Heathrow for the next 8 hours thanks to Flybe, COVID hangover and Brexit – in that order if you want a chronology. In weightage terms, the order would, most likely, be reversed.

In any case, here I am sat, 'sitting' for the punctilious, opposite Harrods Food Hall, wondering if the £12 that Flybe compensated us with would buy me anything there. I haven't checked but I doubt it. If the Caviar and Seafood House right behind me is an indication of food prices at Heathrow, probably not – on the menu is a lobster dish for £65 and with a dash of caviar thrown in, that would be £75, thank you very much.

I didn't ask if I could just have the caviar without the lobster. I don't want to make trouble even before I reach my destination. It has, however, made me ponder over an existentialist conundrum: if someone didn't eat fish but ate eggs, could that person eat caviar, considering caviar is fish (sturgeon) eggs?

Quite a pointless question, of course. But it's a good way to pass time. Only another seven hours to go.

~

60

Privacy? What Privacy?

When a young person falls down, we say they fell – but when it happens to an older person, we say they had a fall. Yesterday evening I had a near fall.

I was going upstairs with a cup of tea in one hand and my iPhone in the other. Halfway up, I stumbled and lost my balance, spilling my tea. I must have cursed aloud, as I'd spilt most of my tea.

My wife, watching TV downstairs, shouted out to me, "Did you fall?"

"No, I just slipped," I replied.

My phone, without any prompting from me, says, "That's what I reckoned."

Yes, my phone spoke without permission – and without the 'Hey Siri' cue.

Incredible? I thought so too. I have heard stories about how the FBI once forced a big company to release all the data it had stored about a dangerous criminal. It seems the company handed over a recording of every bit of sound ever made in his bedroom – including moans, groans and conversations, whether on a call or not.

Immediately after my phone spoke of its own volition, I asked Siri and Alexa whether they were surreptitiously recording me all the time. Both denied it with a vehemence bordering on hurt, and responded by pointing me to their privacy policy which said – you guessed it – they take clients' privacy very seriously - and all that baloney.

Smart devices are getting too smart for my liking.

~

61

Code 100

Why do we treat 'dying' like it's a bad word? Instead of saying someone has died, we resort to all sorts of verbal acrobatics. Inane expressions like 'passed away' or 'passed on' or just 'passed' are in common usage. 'Expired' is a favourite term in India. Life is not a driving test for someone to pass and neither is it a carton of milk to expire. Another word one hears occasionally is departed. As if it were not a human being but a train!

Officialese is no better. Look at accident investigation reports published by governments. "Although the ambulance crew tried their utmost to resuscitate the casualty, he was declared 'life extinct' on arrival at the hospital." And this while concise language is considered de rigueur. Why not just say he was dead on arrival?

When there is a good, clean word for the process, why hide behind euphemisms? When A dies, why not just say A has died. What is so difficult about that?

WhatsApp has taken it to another level. It has removed the last vestige of common sense. There is such a lot of fakery expressed on this platform that I struggle to hold my peace at times. WhatsRight with WhatsApp is the title of the book that I will never write.

Imagine this: someone's elderly father-in-law dies.

Straight to the WhatsApp groups: "My father-in-law died in his sleep. He was 94."

The group is now buzzing with activity. Every man, woman and their dog is writing, writing, writing. Then the deluge.

"Oom Shanthi" accompanied by the obligatory Oom symbol in Devanagari script. Folded hands, mostly brown to match one's skin tone, some sombre white flowers ...

"May his soul rest in peace" accompanied by more emojis.

"God bless his soul" chimes in another, more emojis.

Multiple variations on the God theme. Poor God is overloaded. S/he has been commandeered to look after the departed soul, make sure it is resting peacefully somewhere in the ether, and proffer her/his 'lotus' feet as shelter to the millions of freshly departed souls.

"I am devastated by your loss," writes the more literarily accomplished, able to string a full sentence together. Devastated? Are you real?

Reminds me of the telegram codes we used back in the day. As each telegram was charged by the number of words it contained, one could use economical standard codes that transmitted a standard phrase. Code 100 simply said, "My deep condolences." Neat. Sadly, Indian Telegraphs have abandoned telegrams. @Meta, are you listening? Please introduce standard phraseology. I am drowning in BS. So is God – overworked and drowning in BS.

The one occasion when I couldn't hold my peace, leading to threats of eviction from a WhatsApp group, was when someone's grandmother died and a member consoled the bereaved, "I am sure she is playing in the lap of God."

"She was a grandmother, not a lap dancer," my fingers won the race with my brain and before I knew it, the message was sent and read by the permanent residents of WhatsApp. I still bear the scars of that exchange.

So, next time someone dies and you never even knew this person existed, don't go overboard. Don't send those cheap, overused emojis or those creepy flowers. Just say, "My sincere condolences." Even better, say Code 100.

~

62

Eclipsed by the Rain

Everyone complains about the British weather. "Rains all the time," we whinge. If you ask me, it doesn't rain here, it only leaks. Nevertheless, it has an uncanny knack for preventing the sighting of eclipses, spoiling a game of cricket... I am not complaining about missing last night's lunar eclipse. I am like my cousin's daughter who, on being shown a king cobra slithering through their garden, said, "I can see much better snakes on YouTube." I will see the eclipse another time, another life. If not, I will watch it on YouTube. I won't let the leakage upset me. Go get a life. Call yourself rain? Ha!

If you want to learn from real rain, come to tropical Kerala. There the downpour lasts days. It is intense, full of drama. People dare not step out without an umbrella unless they want holes in their heads. They rather sit on an easy chair with a cup of tea and banana chips to watch the rain. The water gushes down from gutters built into roofs, splashes the gravel covered ground, presses down the trees, and frightens the birds into silence. The sound of water meeting the roof tiles and the hard cemented courtyards - like the crescendo of wedding drums marking the solemn exchange of garlands. Only, the drum beat lasts through the day, the night, and the days following. Spontaneous rivulets coming together in little streams rush to find the lowest level, cascade down streets, down fields, under culverts, ... until they meet the roiling river, the uprooted trees, all travelling at a terrific pace taking some of the earth with it, colouring the water the brown of a milky cup of tea, incessant, unstoppable flow ... real rain. It roars like a lion and sings like a koel - real rain.

Not some feeble dribble of overcast skies absorbed by the dirty mops of grass-covered lawns. Ha! Weak and slimy, Uriah Heep of the heavens, you spoiled my lunar eclipse. I slander you in revenge.

~

63

Parsing

'*Visiting aunts can be a nuisance'* is an example of a sentence that a computer finds hard to process ('parse' in computer speak). Does it mean making the obligatory visit to see an aunt can be a nuisance? Or is it the other way round? Is it a nuisance when an aunt decides to call on you? Whatever it is, the computer struggles and needs context. It needs to parse the sentence not by itself but with some idea of what is being discussed. Context is everything. But then the pundits also say that spoken words achieve only a small percentage of communication.

Poor computer. How it wishes it were human.

Humans are no better though. Just the other day, I was chatting to my ex-tenant in Delhi on WhatsApp. He had vacated my flat last year, and I asked him to check if I owed anything to the electricity company for the period since then – I had received a bill from them. This is how the exchange continued:

"You don't owe anything, zero balance."

"But I have a bill that says I owe some 1000 rupees," I insisted.

"No. I've checked online. You owe nothing."

"OK. In that case, I shouldn't complain."

"Complain? What about? Anyway, here is the link ..."

Poor human. How he wishes he were a computer!

~

64

Jumping to Conclusions

The doctor asked me the other day if I get enough exercise. I told him I jump to conclusions all the time.

And so, the story of my washing machine that trips the electrics at random times. I could have – no, should have – repaired it myself, considering I knew it had to be an earth fault and the culprit (YouTube informed me) is the heating coil – most of the time. However, I had jumped to my first conclusion: to open the machine, I would have to pull it out, and it is such a tight slide fit that I was bound to hurt my back in the process. Then I would have to dismantle the machine, which I have never done before, and then I would have to find the faulty heating coil and order a replacement. So, the machine would be out of commission for several days. Maybe easiest to pay the manufacturer to repair it.

Now, there were two options available to me: pay a small fortune for the first hour and extra for parts, with every further hour chargeable; or cough up one big fortune, parts and labour free irrespective of the time spent.

As I had jumped to the conclusion that the machine needed to be pulled out, I figured the job would take four hours. It was a no-brainer – I went for the second option.

The engineer visited me this morning and, within half an hour, he replaced the heating coil. He didn't have to pull the machine out. The coil was accessible by opening up the front of the machine! So much for my analysis.

This reminds me of a story about an American couple who lost their front door key and called a locksmith company. A young locksmith attended. He broke the lock, did a lot of damage to the door, took three hours and finally opened the door. The couple happily parted with $300. Ten years later, the couple lost their key again and called the same locksmith company. This time, an older locksmith came along and opened the door in five minutes. He demanded $400. The couple were not happy – $400 for a five-minute job? They complained bitterly.

The locksmith then said, "Do you remember, ten years ago, a young locksmith attended your call? Well, I am the same guy. I now have ten years' experience."

And so, I console myself.

~

65

Ambushed by a Book

Boris visits India. He flies directly to Gujarat, the state where Gandhi was born. He aims to strike lucrative deals now that he is no longer shackled by the European Union. He visits Gandhi's Ashram on the banks of the Sabarmati River. He's unaware that Gandhi is no longer in fashion – he has not moved with the times. They present him Gandhi's autobiography, 'My Experiments with Truth.'

"Jolly good," he says. Then adds, "Cor blimey! I must write such a book too."

~

66

The Tyranny of Hope

I saw a mynah bird on Tuesday but couldn't remember how the saying went.

Does it go *one for joy or one for sorrow?* I wondered briefly.

As it turned out, it is indeed one for sorrow, because my day did not end well.

With what hope I transferred my thoughts into a WhatsApp message to my siblings. How wonderful hope is. How devastating when things don't happen as expected. The absurdity of the whole thing – the up and down, elation closely followed by dejection.

Let me copy here what I wrote to my siblings. If nothing else, you will see what I mean by sweet expectation – almost certainty. *What can go wrong? It's all done – just another procedure to complete.*

How wrong I was, and how great my fall was.

Anyway, read the following and I will continue the story in flashback mode. This is like the penultimate scene – not the ending – being screened at the beginning, the story told to explain this scene, and finally, together with the audience, finding out how it ends – if it ends.

—

AM – 25 April, 2022

Amidst the cacophony of the crows, the distant siren of a

train fills me with hope of travel; no – sweet memory of travel. The clack-clack of coaches over the rails, the fresh morning air, the open storybook. No hurry to get anywhere but to enjoy the trip – going back decades, maybe sixty years, to the journey I made on a cool summer morning with my parents to my grandparents' home to spend the school holidays.

Achha din finally aa hee gaya (The good day has finally come). Let us hope everything goes smoothly today.

Say your prayers to your respective gods – that they may smooth the path ahead, remove obstacles however minor, ensure that no last-minute glitches are raised, no creative clerk senses an opportunity to extract some last-minute incidental cash, the registrar has not quarrelled with his wife and does not deliver a googly, some hidden spirits of my parents and ancestors are keeping an eye on things, that I reach in time and the taxi doesn't develop engine trouble or suffer a puncture, no bad omens raise their ugly heads and throw spanners in my works...

I need to pray to someone – to anyone, to everyone – please, please, please. So much rests on the smooth progress of the day. The acha din should not become a *bura din*[8]. I'll do anything to get over today.

If I were the praying type, I would be ringing bells and showering petals and smearing my forehead with every holy unguent – ash and vermilion and sandalwood paste. I would be standing with folded hands in deep supplication. I would be sending mental petitions to temples in all four corners with vows of circumambulation flat on my back, vows of total tonsure, pledges of offering the equivalent of my weight in

---

8 *Bura din, bad days*

bananas and coconuts, trips to Benares and Kailas. I would offer milk and bananas to serpent gods who need neither, pledge to feed a hundred and one orphans, do a month's *seva*[9] at the gurdwara, go to Mecca, get blessings from the Pope, bang my head on the Wailing Wall of Jerusalem...

But I, being a nothing-believer, can only sit here and worry – ruminate rather ruefully that my journey is coming to an end, like the end of train journeys that I had always hoped would last just a bit longer.

I will miss the clack-clack rattle of the journey, the opportunistic obstructors and the bribe-seeking clerks and the officials who demand my grandfather's birth certificate just to make my life a little more difficult. I will miss these – but I won't look back wistfully and wish for them.

—

PM – 25 April, 2022

It didn't happen! All the computer servers were down and so everyone was told to go home. I have forfeited my return flight to London and will try again. The next appointment is at 13.24 on 27 April 2022. Surely, the acha din must come eventually.

—

PM – 27 April, 2022

The server was returned after repairs but is refusing to play. Net effect? I am stuck in Delhi, slowly roasting in the 44°C heat.

—

9 *Seva: Service carried out with devotion*

PM – 29 April, 2022

The server is working. My heart is beating faster, I am ebullient, full of hope.

And I did see two mynahs last evening.

~

67

Noise Festival

The crows start at the break of dawn. Dogs are late risers and are used to the incessant cawing. They slumber on. People start waking up. Cars and two-wheelers are soon in motion. The garbage collection van from the municipality is getting ready for action. It's generating several decibels with its double-toned alarm. It sounds as if someone is breaking into the vehicle. The irony of stealing from a garbage van is puzzling. A quick glance resolves the mystery. The vehicle sounds a siren while reversing. Safety first – close your ears if you can't bear the noise. The crows, unable to compete with the van, take off en masse from the Asoka tree across the road. They settle down when it stops reversing and resume their relentless din.

The dogs, still having a lie-in – under cars, on top of cars – have no choice but to wake up. They bark randomly at the emerging day as if asking each other what the day has in store for them. A few elderly residents get together for their morning meditation. They finish with synchronised *Oom* chanting. "Oom Oom Oom," they invoke the Universal Consciousness. The dogs find this irresistible and join in. Ooo Ooo Ooo they howl. Their friends pick up the signal from far corners until the whole place is reverberating with their primordial wolf howl. Caw caw caw – the crows keep up their dissonant chorus. Just then a call to prayer from a distant mosque – the azan seems fainter than I remembered. Am I imagining it or has the general noise level increased?

The garbage van kicks into action.

"A clean India, yes, a clean India, together we will build a clean India," the recorded song plays out, full blast. Maids (Little People) carry their masters' garbage in plastic bags and throw them in the van. A man (Little People) is riding on the bumper guard and sorts the garbage in real time. Aluminium cans and bottles in one section, paper in another ...

Enter the fruit and vegetable sellers (Little People).

"Buy potatoes, buy tomatoes, buy mangoes ... ," they list their wares in no particular order.

House owners query the price from their second and third-floor apartments. An elderly lady is scandalised by the price of mangoes.

"90 rupees for one mango? Hai Ram! This is robbery," she berates the vendor. When she gets no response, she changes her tone.

"Will you take 80?"

"It's morning time. Can't refuse the first sale. You're killing a poor man. Anyway ..." he concedes with a shrug. He has a smug smile tucked away under his bushy moustache. To the world, he's the exploited underdog. The lady comes down and buys a dozen. She too is hiding a smile under her chunni, which she uses as a semi-veil. No one else bargains, for the price has been publicly declared and agreed, at least for the day. Mangoes sell out in no time. The vendor throws a ripe tomato to a dog, and it smacks its lips in gratitude.

A crow perches on the gate and looks sideways with longing at the ripe tomatoes. No such luck for the bird. It has no status. It finds no mention in any of the religious tomes.

Not even the vehicle of a minor god. No legendary antics associated with it. Unlike the squirrel who gained his stripes by helping Sri Rama build his bridge to Lanka, by rolling in the mud and unrolling at the other end, the crow can claim nothing. It is the bird equivalent of persona non grata. The fruit seller shoos it away. Oh! Never to be born a crow, ever.

A car honks. It is parked on the side. A driver (Little People) is at the wheel. Drivers don't dare honk for their lords and masters. A few minutes later he honks again as if testing it still works. He looks bored. He sits there honking at regular intervals until lunchtime.

The curtains are all drawn, the ceiling fan spins, slicing the warm air a thousand times a minute. The air conditioner whirs in the corner, competing with the fan, inserting slices of cold air into the room. The external noises are muffled. Then suddenly there is an ear-piercing loud tune – JINGLE BELLS JINGLE BELLS JINGLE ALL TH... – it is either a reversing vehicle or Christmas come too early. A peep through the curtains confirms the reversing vehicle theory.

I fall asleep and dream of dogs, mangoes, Christmas, mass uprising of the Little People, crows raising the slogans of revolution – thereby securing a place for themselves in the annals of this nation ... among other things.

~

68

An Open Letter to My Cycle Thief

20 March, 2019

Dear Cycle Thief,

Hope you are enjoying my bike – or the parts of it that you couldn't sell. If you've offloaded it in the nether market, I hope the money bought you a few pleasures. But I'm straying from the point now. Digressing – if you understand the word. No aspersion on your education, just a thought that occurred to me. In your profession, you cannot afford to digress. You cannot head for the bike shed with your chain cutters and suddenly entertain an alternative thought, like: "Let me check out the magnolia tree. Its blossoms are so overwhelmingly beautiful this time of year." No. You must be the master of concentration. One-track minded. A Zen of bicycle thievery.

I'm being given a replacement bike – after winning long and tedious arguments with the insurance company. I really wished I had your phone number, because they wanted a photograph of the stolen bicycle, and I could have asked you to text me one. You could have been in the photo too, complete with your hoodie masking your ugly face. I assume it's ugly, because then the hoodie would be doing you a double favour, wouldn't it? Granted, some thieves are good-looking – but they're in a different league. They wear ill-fitting Savile Row suits, crocodile-skin shoes, and millstone necklaces. They don't steal bicycles. They steal entire nations.

I meant to ask – before placing my order for the replacement bike – would you like a mountain bike, a cyclo-cross, or a road bike? It's better you state your preference now, because the last two bikes I gave you were obviously not good enough. Would you prefer one of those folding bikes? Much easier to steal. But sadly, like guide dogs, they're allowed inside office buildings. So, you're screwed there. Anyway, let me know. Would you like lights and some mudguards too? I hate spinning muck off the road onto my clothes and going around looking like I'd been lashed for a crime I hadn't committed.

Oh, by the way – the police are not interested. Looks like they've struck bicycle theft off their list of crimes. So continue to steal without fear, with impunity. In fact, I am seriously considering your profession. It's nearly risk-free. Very little effort required. As long as I put my black hoodie on and don't smile for the CCTV cameras, I'm sorted.

"See, it could be anyone," the police said.

"We don't have a camera pointing directly at the bike shed," our building security said.

"My neighbour's £3,000 bike was stolen just the other day," my boss said.

It was supposed to make me feel better. After all, my bike was worth only a third of that. Never mind. Like they (I) say: look beyond words; look at intention. Please don't think I'm name-dropping to wind you up – or to make you feel you've wasted your efforts on a cheap bicycle when there was a better one for the picking. Or dare I say, *unpicking?* I tell you all this with an ulterior motive. Read on – I have a plan.

"You have an excess of £250," the insurance company said.

"Collect it from my thief," I responded.

I couldn't quite figure out why the line went dead after that.

You won't believe this. The insurance company was offering me a bike 30% cheaper than ours. (I hope you don't mind my using the possessive plural here. The least you can do is share the ownership with me – on paper, at least.) Granted, you own it now. But we didn't exactly sign an ownership transfer form like the DVLA's V5C.

In fact, this could be a good business model, come to think of it. Knowing that the police, the building security, and everyone else who matters don't really care, it's worth considering. Yes, this idea is developing legs. I wanted to say wheels, but then you stole my wheels, didn't you.

Do you offer any training? Have you got a website on the dark web? Or a YouTube channel? If you don't, start one now – or publish an instruction manual: *How to Steal a Bike from Idiots, for Idiots*. See? I even gave you a catchy title. Seriously, shall we start a partnership? I could be your frontman – your agent, so to speak. You give me a percentage for every bike you steal, and I give some of that to the insurance company to cover the excess. Now that would really work.

Anyway, enjoy my bike – if you still have it. Don't worry if you're getting tired of it and ready for a change. A brand-spanking-new one is on its way. Yes, the locks will be stronger this time. But hey – like they say, locks are for gentlemen.

~

69

Thalassery

To be astounded by the sights and sounds one grew up with is an odd feeling. The distance, both temporal and spatial, between me and my childhood works in my favour. I'm like a tourist staring with open-mouthed wonder at the exploding greenery as the summer rain washes it clean. The disproportionately large banana leaf, as long as the trunk of its tree; bright yellow jackfruit hanging precariously at impossible angles; proud coconut trees standing tall like benevolent guardians; the rain serenading a steady lullaby; and the throaty music of birds. I'm in God's Own Country, in the town I was born: Thalassery.

~

70

Chaos in the Canal

I have pontificated *ad nauseam* on maritime safety in my career as an Inspector of Marine Accidents. There was, however, one occasion when I became the victim of a marine accident. It could have killed me. In any case, I die with shame each time I remember the event.

My family and I decided to take a holiday in Kumarakom, Kerala, at the southern tip of the Indian subcontinent. A place of unspoilt natural beauty, it boasts expansive freshwater lagoons and pristine rainforests. With its tropical climate, Kerala was nothing less than ideal for a holiday. No wonder the travel brochures call it 'God's own country'. I was born there and speak Malayalam, the local language. I was a tourist, but I was also coming home.

We arrived late in the evening and checked into a resort on the shore of the grand Vembanad lake. The plan was to stay there for a few days and spend a couple of days on a houseboat. Around fifty cottages dotted the banks of a grid of canals fed by water from the lake. The verdant tropical flora was canopied by lanky coconut trees, some stooping so low as if to kiss the water. A raft of ducklings caused the placid surface to ripple and shimmer in the warm morning sunshine. Hibiscus blooms – red, white, and yellow – endowed the gardens with luxuriant abundance. I slipped into a nostalgic trance, my senses soaking in the familiar sights and smells. The evocative double note of a koel's call completed the picture.

Noticing a canoe moored along the canal bank, I proposed that we take it for a paddle. My family refused to join me; however, my prescient wife offered to look after my newly acquired camera if I decided to venture out on a solo expedition. Slipping the boat from its mooring, I navigated the canals, expertly manoeuvring the craft in full and admiring view of the guests. I basked in the attention. Paddling with the languid ease of a seasoned boatman, I enjoyed a sense of wellbeing.

A young couple sipped their morning tea in the veranda of their cottage. Their son, about ten years old, watched deferentially as if I were the master of *Queen Mary 2* navigating the Dardanelles passage.

The mother locked eyes with me and said, "Looks like you know what you're doing!"

I was pleased with her comment. As a marine engineer, I fixed engines, boilers, and other items of machinery. I knew very little about navigation and did not know the first thing about small boats. But then, did she need to know such details? Moreover, how much could I say as I glided by?

I replied, a touch patronisingly, "Spent fifteen years at sea. I should know what I am doing!"

I could see undiluted admiration in her eyes. She was, perhaps, experiencing some vicarious pleasure observing my boating skills. Then, without the slightest warning and directly in front of them, the canoe capsized. I found myself under the boat, trying not to ingest or inhale the brackish green water. The canal wasn't deep, and I managed to stand up, but was anchored firmly to the mud. I couldn't move without abandoning my shoes. Lips sealed in a tight grimace and chin raised to prevent inhalation of water, I stood there, water lapping just below my nose. To onlookers, I must have seemed oddly proud of my mishap. I was a spectacle, a pantomime of the ancient mariner minus his ship. Dozens of eyes widened simultaneously in concern.

Lifeguards came to my rescue and extracted me, my canoe and its paddle from the water. Hotel employees and guests gathered to offer their analyses of the capsize. Some mollifying remarks about the poor design of the boat were floated. It must have been an undercurrent that caught me out: another explanation. I was grateful for their generosity. Nevertheless, I felt eminently foolish.

I had to deliver the boat back to its mooring. Squinting through algae-coated glasses, I paddled, seated in a pool of water collected from my dripping clothes. People watched, more in amusement than admiration. The young mother did her best to look concerned as I rowed past her cottage once again. She masked her smile behind her teacup, but her eyes betrayed her – she was cracking up inside.

At dinner, we met the family. They were polite and refrained from discussing my morning misadventure. However, their son had other ideas. Despite the parents' stern looks and the forbidding 'don't you dare' Indian nod, he approached our table with a twinkle in his eyes.

"Uncle," he addressed me using the endearing term, "it was so funny this morning. After your boat turned over, you stood like a statue in the water! Sooo funny!" He then performed a little skit of me emerging from under the canoe and standing with my chin above the water. I have been fortunate to have the ability to laugh at myself, sometimes, too readily.

By then, I was refreshed and dressed in clean, dry clothes. A skinful of fresh coconut palm toddy helped speed my recovery.

I responded, "Son, would you like some canoeing lessons?"

The parents, initially embarrassed by their son's antics, burst out in relieved laughter.

We raised our glasses - *To safety.*

~

71

The Technology of Ice

Father moved his law practice from the District Court in Thalassery to the High Court in Ernakulam. His friend had loaned us his house while we looked for accommodation. The friend had tasked his maid to look after us while he was away during the summer holidays.

The trees in the back garden, weighed down with ripe fruits, caught our early attention. There was a guava tree just outside the kitchen. We had never seen so many guavas on one tree – not even in Kunnoth, our ancestral land in the foothills of the Western Ghats.

The fecundity of this Eden of Ernakulam was short-lived. Like locusts, we stripped the tree bare on the first day. The maid sat helplessly in a corner, right hand on her upper forehead, observing us with open-mouthed astonishment. She was wrinkled and white-haired. She didn't know that the antics of the feral bunch of kids who invaded her normally staid household would age her further in the weeks that followed.

While our parents were out house-hunting, we set about exploring the house. A refrigerator was as alien to us in 1965 as a spaceship from Mars would be to you today. We explored it with wonderment and a sense of adventure.

Everything was so cool inside, in contrast to the sweltering summer temperatures. But what was that compartment on the top? It was really cold and contained ice. I had seen ice once earlier in Thalassery, when a large block of it – covered in sawdust – was brought home in an old gunny bag. But here the ice was so clean. The tray was full of little ice blocks, and there was no sawdust to be seen anywhere. No gunny bag either.

With difficulty I pried the tray out of the compartment and smelt it. Nothing. Well, it must taste of something then. I put my tongue under the tray and it got stuck. I panicked and screamed as loudly as one could without the use of a tongue. An older sibling came to my rescue and yanked the tray with all her might. It released, possibly taking a piece of my tongue with it. It stung for a few minutes. But now we had the ice tray – without any means to get the ice out.

We never thought of asking the maid, having ignored her presence at the outset.

We were focused on the task at hand. We needed to get the ice out of its tray. Someone brought a machete from the kitchen while the maid cowered in the corner. She was mumbling to herself, *"Endeeswara!"* (Oh my God). We attacked the tray with the machete until ice cubes and shavings of aluminium scattered on the kitchen floor. The smooth red cement floor, too, took a few blows and disintegrated in places, colouring the ice cubes a bloody red.

We washed the ice cubes and ate them, crunching them with our strong teeth, swallowing them whole and relishing their difficult, icy passage down to our stomachs. We jettisoned the ice tray in the backyard. The maid, muttering incoherently, retrieved the tray, washed it, filled it with water, and put it back in the refrigerator.

The next morning, there was brand new ice gleaming invitingly from its dented tray. It was only then that we understood the technology behind turning boring old water into delightful ice!

~

72

The Black-and-White Dog

I am in Delhi, the city of my youth.

"Be careful," cautions Maya, the live-in housekeeper. I had known her when she was a young schoolgirl. She is now a mother of three girls in their twenties. Two of her front teeth are missing, like missing milestones marking the passage of time – some forty years.

"Be careful of the dogs, big brother," she warns me.

From the balcony I see hordes of strays roaming the streets. They are mongrels, predominantly fawn, but there are some black-and-white ones as well. They settle canine scores with sporadic fights but, on the whole, are peaceful.

I am unable to access my local bank account online. Maya tells me the landline is not working and so the internet is down as well.

"I will go and tell the man to fix it," she says.

I ask if the man is to be found at the phone provider's office.

"There is no office," she smiles. "He just hangs around in the market in the mornings."

She finds him later and tells him to fix the phone line. The man promises to come round but doesn't turn up.

"I will try again tomorrow," says Maya, who is quite used to such truant behaviour. I have lost my Indian stoicism after nearly thirty years of living abroad and frown with impatience.

I open the gate and step outside the apartment building. The youngest of the three *chowkidars* (security guards) asks me, "Where are you going, big brother?"

A question that would be considered too direct anywhere else.

"To the bank," I reply calmly, because I know he means well and his question is only a preamble to providing me with some unsolicited advice. With a look I couldn't quite place and a nod that said, 'Wait, don't go away,' he disappears behind the building. I may have lost my subtle nods but haven't forgotten their nuanced meanings. He brings me a bamboo staff, about twice the length of a walking stick.

"If you keep this with you, the dogs won't bite" he says, handing me the staff.

"However," the second chowkidar cautions, "the black-and-white dog doesn't like sticks."

Holding the staff in my right hand extended in front and resembling a biblical shepherd, I venture out. Some dogs are sunning themselves on the roof of parked cars, and some are sleeping under the cars.

My rupee debit card has stopped working because I haven't used it for a while.

"Just go to your local branch and they will issue you an instant debit card," a stranger waiting to use the ATM gives me free advice.

I walk to my local branch, stick in hand.

Yes, I am told by my bank, an instant debit card can be

issued, but I need to apply online. But I don't have access to the internet since I'm still waiting for the man with no office. I return, waving my stick at the strays and promptly hiding it behind my back the instant I spot a black-and-white dog. Reaching home with neither cash nor incident, I sleep off my jet lag.

I wake up to a clamour outside. A Good Samaritan has come with food for the strays, but a local resident objects to the feeding. They argue loudly. Several others join in and soon it is a shouting match between pro-dog (dog-walleh, as Maya calls them) and anti-dog groups. The dogs gather in a rough circle around the feuding neighbours. They observe with an almost supercilious air, silent and dignified observers of the human charade. A man tilts his head sideways at a black-and-white dog, not daring to point at her directly.

"She has bitten twenty-one people so far."

The bitch wags her tail at those who dare glance in her direction.

"Who? Me? Bite? Never!" Her limpid grey eyes protest her innocence.

I don't find out who wins the argument. My friend arrives to take me for dinner. He explains the reason for the proliferation of dogs in Delhi. The government minister in charge of animal welfare has banned the killing of stray dogs. Her solution is to neuter them. My friend tells me how everyone drives, even two houses down the road, because of their fear of being bitten. That is, everyone who can afford a car, not the little people. The little people, he adds in verbal parentheses, include maids, chowkidars, drivers, cooks, gophers, ironing people, vegetable sellers, gardeners, hangers-on, and visiting relatives of the little people. I remind him I am no foreign tourist and have grown up in Delhi. I know who the little people are and why they remain little. I am incensed by the social disparities in my native land, I tell him.

"OK, OK! Let's stick to dogs," my friend stops me midstream.

I think about my day: lots of running around, more wise counsel than I could wag a staff at, broken promises, circular arguments, and dog fights. And a fight about dogs. Yes, I am home!

My wife, Sujata, and I are back in Delhi some three months later. The dogs roam free and there is a litter of five pups living in the park opposite our apartment. They appear hungry and cold, and sleep piled on top of each other for warmth. They resemble a post-modern art installation.

Sujata, devoid of any fear of dogs, strokes their foreheads and talks to them. She refuses to carry a stick. The deadly black-and-white dog seems to have changed her character or is just overwhelmed by the kindness. Her grey eyes smile. She nuzzles up to my wife, wagging her bushy tail in grateful appreciation.

Some dogs are allowed into the dog-walleh's homes to spend the night but are ejected at daybreak so as not to upset the anti-dog-walleh. A passer-by stops and talks to one of them. It sounds like he is cooing to a baby. The dogs continue to be fed, surreptitiously and in darkness. There is a non-governmental organisation (NGO) that looks after their welfare. They are funded by a section of the community who believe that the first chapati of the day should go to the cow and the last to the dog.

At nightfall, a young employee of the NGO arrives on a bicycle laden with baskets of food. He lays down newspapers at the side of the road and feeds the dogs rice and chicken. They are happy and come alive, energised by the meal. My sleep is punctuated by their collective barking. Their synchronised howl melds with the deliberate sounds generated by the chowkidar. The sound of his bamboo staff crashing on the tarmac every few minutes, and the piercing screech of his whistle, transport me to my school days.

"I am awake. I am alert," he transmits his message to thieves and other undesirable elements of the night. "Go, make your mischief somewhere else."

The dogs don't do him the courtesy of opening their eyes. They are in deep slumber, probably dreaming of warmth and food. I step out onto the balcony and marvel at the serene night. Compared to the mayhem of the day, the change seems metamorphic. It is the Delhi I know. Nothing much has changed, yet everything feels different.

Day breaks. A chauffeur in white uniform, complete with a peaked cap and white buckskin shoes, is waiting for his employers to emerge from their mansion. Bored with waiting, he goes around beating random dogs with a stick. He has a sinister smile on his face and the dogs yelp in surprised pain. I shout at him from my balcony and ask him how he would feel if I were to go down and beat him with a stick. His make-believe world of a tiger-hunting Maharaja is shattered. He stops hurting the dogs. I go to the bathroom and cry.

Maya tells me the story of an entire litter of six being run over by a car. From that day, the heartbroken black-and-white mother started biting passers-by. I console myself this is a fabricated tale, for I couldn't contemplate the horrific alternative of it being true. Like everything in the country of my birth, things are not as they appear to be. There are layers of meaning to everything, and every story has a moral. Before long, someone will build a shrine, on our street in Delhi, dedicated to a black-and-white dog. Fact and myth will merge and dog-walleh and anti-dog-walleh will pay obeisance to her, ring a bell, and say a prayer. Of this, I am certain.

~

73

The Magic Potion

I discovered the secret of *Holi* as a marine engineering student in Calcutta. *Holi* is a North Indian festival that marks the triumph of good over evil, the herald of spring. Total strangers on the streets daub each other with colour, embrace and exchange sweets. Shy individuals shed their inhibitions for the day, becoming loud and boisterous. Children ambush adults with missiles of small water-filled balloons. No one complains and the bonhomie is pervasive. Being a South Indian I was ignorant of some of the dubious traditions of *Holi* that could explain the altered public behaviour.

One cool Sunday morning in the month of March, my roommate shakes me awake. "Let's celebrate *Holi*," he says.

I don't ask if it isn't too early in the day to party. We make our way down to the ground floor of the student accommodation. A large stainless steel drum brimming with a milky white drink is placed at the centre of the courtyard. People mill around, the waiters making sure their glasses are never empty. It is an eclectic gathering: officers in starched white uniforms and peaked caps embellished with decorations resembling scrambled eggs, young wives of officers in white chiffon sarees, fresh-faced cadets ogling the women's bosoms, clerks and peons smelling of moth-eaten files and mildew, waiters, mess-boys, cooks, gardeners. Everyone is cheerful and engages with those around them. The class hierarchy of India and the strict discipline of our semi-naval academy have been replaced with an egalitarian milieu.

The intriguing fragrance of the drink assails my senses. I sample my first glass. I have never tasted anything so exquisite – it is imbued with the richness of almonds and pistachio, sweetness of sugarcane, and the mystery of Kashmiri saffron. Sweets wrapped in edible silver form the perfect complement to the drink. I have a second glass, a third ... I stop counting.

A friend, usually reserved and introverted, is streaking in the corridors. Why would he do that in front of all the women? But where are the women? I cannot see them anymore, nor the officers in uniform. It was 9 a.m. when I glanced at my watch a few minutes ago and now it is 2 p.m! What did I do in the interregnum? What is happening to my sense of time? My thoughts are random and pile up like an unsteady stack of plates. Then I couldn't hear myself. Am I talking or just thinking?

There is colour everywhere, both dry and wet. Peacock blues, vermilion reds and marigold yellows, as if a mad artist has painted a spring cloud. I am caught in the thrall of celebration. Someone empties a bucket of coloured water on my head, and I shiver in shocked surprise.

"Holi hai, Holi mubarak!" "It is *Holi, Happy Holi,*" the revellers shout. The drum of the milky drink is constantly being replenished. Everyone's glasses are full.

Disembodied mouths bare their teeth in glee through the coloured air. All of a sudden, a spiral staircase materialises in front of me. In place of banisters, it has rows of diamonds. They are intertwined like mating snakes, and disappear into infinite space. The bright sun enhances their iridescence, and I stare with open-mouthed wonder. I step on the stairs to grab the jewels, but they remain tantalisingly out of reach. I climb the stairs; it feels like an eternal journey. The distant music from a shehnai enters my head and reverberates inside. The music ends and the staircase vanishes. Someone refills my glass.

A classmate is weeping, unable to stop. I join in, weeping in empathy, although I don't know the cause of his distress. I am like a harmonium, a mellifluous but dull accompaniment to the main act. My friend stops crying. Like the sun emerging after a thunder burst, his mood changes instantly. He is now laughing, bent over, clutching his stomach. I laugh with him. Others join us, and we laugh as if we are part of a group laughter therapy session – only our mirth is genuine.

We become serious again and explore the connection of western existentialism with our homegrown Advaita or nonduality. We argue passionately about the inseparability of God and man. We are young, barely familiar with these lofty concepts. Yet, we believe we are philosophers. Then, someone tells a silly joke and we roll on the ground in merriment. As we laugh, we cry some. The tears that flow from our eyes belong to both sorrow and joy, indistinguishable from each other or the cosmic spirit: Advaita in practice.

I pose my favourite conundrum to my friends – if you see a rope and jump in fear, mistaking it for a snake, does the rope still exist? We debate this: there is no rope, only snake. No, there is no snake, only rope. We argue with passion. The snake is illusory, lives only in our mind. It is the embodiment of our fear, I explain, imparting the wisdom of a sage. Then I recoil in horror. Hooded serpents stand on their tails, poised, ready to strike, forked tongues – little slivers of pink – darting in and out, mesmerising eyes freezing me in a hypnotic trance. I am helpless, and my head sways as I follow their minute movements. Death knocks. I weep, overcome by a primeval fear, and say my goodbyes, pointing at the venomous reptiles surrounding me.

My friends laugh and ask, "Snakes? What snakes?" Only then do the creatures disappear. I am alive.

I find myself on the third floor. I am convinced I can fly and attempt to scale the parapet. My friends restrain me. In my head, I am falling into that unending void once again.

"Call the doctor," I plead, "I cannot bear this anymore." My friend runs to the campus medic's residence, but returns alone. He is carrying a message from the doctor.

"Sorry. Today, I too am very high. Tell Gopi to stay off the bhang[10]."

~

---

10 Bhang, a preparation made from the leaves and flowers of the cannabis plant. It has been traditionally consumed in India for centuries, especially during festivals like Holi and Maha Shivaratri.

74

The Indian Marine Engineer

RTFM (Read the F***ing Manual) is a well-known abbreviation used by marine engineers. In my opinion, it should be RTFMP – P for *properly*. I'm beginning to understand what M. Biswas, the Strength of Materials lecturer back in my DMET (Directorate of Marine Engineering Training) days, used to say: "DMET is a hollow pipe. You come in from one end and you get out from the other."

Otherwise, why would I mix up the positive and negative terminals of the car battery? Yes, the positive was not marked red, but there was an embossed '+' sign next to it and – if you looked carefully – a '–' sign next to the other. Okay, my eyesight is not what it used to be, and I operate from memory these days. My memory is not the same as it used to be, either. I'm getting the feeling that I'm repeating myself. But such is life – a repetitive degradation of faculties, gradual but certain.

Anyway, I'll get to the point.

I had to take my wife to the hospital for a 12:30 appointment. When I clicked the open switch on my key, nothing happened. My 15-year-old car let me down for the first time. The battery had drained completely, and I knew the cause: of late, the radio wouldn't turn off and I was too lazy to sort it out. I knew there was a fault somewhere, and all I had to do was disconnect the negative terminal and reconnect it.

I am not as sprightly or energetic as I used to be (again): procrastination has become my companion. *Why do something today, when tomorrow lies empty?*

I didn't have time to even call a taxi. Luckily, David, my neighbour – a retired hospital consultant – came to our rescue and drove us to the hospital.

On returning home, I set about fixing the car. But as I am lazy, I tried the AA first.

"We can only do home calls tomorrow," said the man who answered, remorse in his voice. He couldn't answer the basic question: "Then why am I paying you every month?"

Left with no option, I decided to diagnose and repair.

Opening a bonnet is easy – but not in my car. It, like me – or like a faithful dog – was ageing, and the two of us had our minor quirks we had learned to live with.

After releasing the clasp from inside the car, one has to tug at a piece of plastic that protrudes through the front grill. This piece had broken, and I'd substituted it with a cable tie; it worked perfectly if pulled at an upward angle. But, not having had many occasions to open the bonnet, I'd forgotten about the angled pull.

Eventually, the cable tie broke. An hour and a couple of bent screwdrivers later, I managed to release the bonnet. By then I was tired and frustrated – and angry.

This is probably why I momentarily mixed up the battery terminals. Extracting a battery charger from my garage, I connected it up – plus to minus and minus to plus. BAM!

Red light on the charger under the label 'Connection wrong, replace fuse'.

Now this whole episode was beginning to get on my nerves.

As if on cue, Bumble, the neighbourhood cat, appeared at that exact moment and perched on my battery. This was an added distraction I did not want. So I sent a picture of the delinquent cat to the neighbourhood WhatsApp group – it elicited a lot of wisecracks, puns, and metaphors.

I struggled on, hoping the cat would either get electrocuted or be taken away by its owner. Eventually, the owner turned up. Uncharacteristic of the British, he didn't apologise but just kept saying thank you, as the cat purred like a newborn in his arms. I ignored the pair of them.

I should have eaten something and rested a bit before continuing. But I was focused on the job, and the hospital was expected to call to pick up my wife after her surgery. I didn't want to ask David again, although he had offered another lift if required. My pride was at stake.

The beauty of the Indian marine engineer, as Biswas said, was that we managed – we got things done – somehow, anyhow.

I needed a 20A fuse to get my charger working. I knew there was a fuse box in the boot under the first-aid kit. A quick look at the manual, and I spotted the words 'Spare fuses' on the diagram and convinced myself that the entire box of fuses and relays tucked away in the boot was a spare set.

When you're panicking, you convince yourself of anything as long as it looks like a solution.

I pulled out a 20A fuse and got the charger working. Plus to plus, minus to the car body – the charger was working.

Half an hour of fast-charge and a multimeter reading of 11.6V later, I disconnected the charger and turned the ignition. The engine turned but didn't fire. It was as if it was not getting any fuel.

The manual made some vague reference to a fuse layout diagram to be found in one of the fuse boxes near the driver's seat.

I turned to YouTube.

The 20A fuse I had pulled out was not a spare one. It was for the fuel pump.

By then, the battery had died again – and another hour of charging, fuse back in its original slot, and the car started.

Beethoven's *Moonlight Sonata* didn't sound as sweet.

The hospital called late that night.

Thinking about it, I could have just left the car and called a taxi.

But the Indian marine engineer in me was out to prove that, despite my poor eyesight, my fading memory, and my rapidly depleting energy levels, I had not passed through a hollow pipe.

Did I hear you say that I should replace my car?

How dare you!

~

75

Of Kittens, Roses and Grandchildren

In November last year, we planted thirty *Rosa Rugosas* in our front garden. Our house faces east. All the plants in the southeast quadrant are thriving, but those in the northeast are languishing. Three of them have died and the other twelve are just about surviving. No one – not even the Royal Horticultural Society (RHS) – is able to diagnose the malaise. It is high up in my list of annoyances, like grit in the shoe.

I am pulling out some weeds growing in the shelter of the roses when a woman comes round asking if I've seen four missing kittens. They've gone missing from her neighbour's garden, immediately backing on to mine. Did I see any of them in my garden?

"No."

"What about that garden?" She points at the house to my southwest.

"They are away on holiday."

"Do you think they would mind if I had a quick look?"

"I'm sure they won't," I said, not at all sure. "I'll come with you."

We enter my holidaying neighbour's back garden and look for the lost kittens. Nothing. I am now in a quandary – should I join the woman in her hunt for the lost kittens? Is that what is expected of a good neighbour? I don't know, and I decide to go back to pulling weeds.

The owner of the kittens turns up. He informs me the mother of the lost kittens is from Bulgaria. Then we start talking about his ski resort in Bulgaria, and his cottage by the Black Sea. I experience traces of envy.

Another neighbour opens her front door. She doesn't recognise the Bulgarian and thinks he is selling kitchens, when he asks,

"Have you seen some kittens?"

The lost kittens are not foremost in his mind, and he is confident they will eventually return. He goes away, and I am reassured – if the owner is not panicking, I am not duty bound to hunt for kittens. I pull more weeds.

Then someone asks if I have checked my pond, and I worry. The goldfish in my pond don't show any sign of having encountered kittens in their patch.

"Will they drown?" I ask her, hoping she would tell me otherwise.

"They will drown," she says mercilessly.

I take another look at my pond. The goldfish stare back, stoic as ever.

The ice cream van announces itself with its loud but welcome tune. An entire family including five grandchildren emerge. The sight elates me: the look of expectant delight in the children's eyes, the simple elegance of a happy family. The lost kittens are temporarily forgotten, and I think wistfully, I too should have been a grandfather. I feel a bit sad, but it passes. No point worrying about the past when the present itself is so fragile.

Some more concerned neighbours appear. One goes about

calling, "Katooch, Katooch." I ask her what she means. She tells me about her ex-boyfriend who is from ex-Czechoslovakia. He had a cat that he called 'Katooch', which was Czech for cat. I told her about the man from Kerala who declared: English is a funny language. They write C-A-T but pronounce K-A-T, when it really means *poocha* – cat in Malayalam.

It's 6 p.m. Everyone is busy with their dinners. Will the kittens return? Will the roses in the northeast quadrant survive? Will I too have a grandchild one day? Questions I grapple with all in the course of a single day.

The kittens were eventually found. They were hiding within the upholstery of a chair and had never left home.

~

76

Monty G

My dearest Monty G, you left us today. If there is a dog heaven, you must be there already. If you didn't get in, then I don't know who will. A sweeter dog than you there never was. Will I walk you tomorrow? Who will notice a man walking an absent dog? No one. I will have your brown lead dangling from my pocket. I will carry your favourite biscuits and I will whistle for you. I will do this every morning, rain or snow or Christmas. For you insist on your walks, and now I cannot just stop. I will not remember you are no more. I will shout your name in the woods and other dog owners will roll their eyes and smile. "Labradors," they would say. "Yes, Labradors!" I would concur and roll my eyes in reply and, ever so surreptitiously, wipe a tear.

I will not paint the wall or polish the floor at home to erase the dark patches where you snuggled. I will not throw away your bed or remove it from the landing – the bed that you chewed to make your own. I see you contorting your huge body into the little space under my desk, the space you claim as your own and insist on occupying. "Go write somewhere else," you say.

I will keep you alive. To me, Monty G, you are not dead. You have just gone missing, and you will answer my whistling. It's time to pick up mum from the bus stop. Come on. Let's go. You will raise your moist nose and wag your tail when you spot her at a distance. You will then pretend not to have seen her when she is close. Such a wind-up artist you are!

Your brother is weeping, mum is weeping too, but I have no tears because, to me, you are only missing. Gone to find that tasty piece of sandwich someone has jettisoned into the bush. You know you have to return to me when you sense I am too far away for comfort, when your metric of separation is exceeded. You will abandon your tasty morsel and return reluctantly, casting wistful backward glances at what you had to forego.

Your smell lingers at home. The water bowl is full. There is a full meal on your plate. All you need to do is turn up now. You may tap me with your paws and threaten to climb into bed if you don't get your walk on time. Please, just once, you need to bark in that complaining, whining sort of fashion. Neither angry nor nasty, just impatient.

And it's not even the weekend. It is Friday. You won't let me have a lie-in like you let me on Saturdays, Sundays and bank holidays. You know a lot more than you let on. Your barks get increasingly more frequent, stubbornly insistent. You drool through the gaps in your teeth and eventually, I accept defeat and succumb to your bullying.

So, yes. Monty G, you are missing. That's all. We are walking in the woods. Just me and your brown lead, and a missing chocolate lab. You smile down at me from dog heaven as I whistle: shoooeee phoooeeee shoooeee. The metric of separation has long been overshot. You need to come back. You must. Please.

~

77

Indian Emotions

It is a curious feeling, one I cannot put my finger on, that I experience every time I return to India. I curse and spit venom at the chaos and confusion, the lost courier packages, the cancelled flights, the proliferation of stray dogs who rule the streets because of their protected status, flaunting the dusty winter coats some Good Samaritans have forced upon them (with entirely selfish motives of enhancing their Karma accounts and not out of any compassion for the animals), the mysterious workings of the courts with lawyers wearing frayed black coats and collar bands soliciting for business at every turn, judges offering off the record advice on how to get things done the quick way.

Then I stare in wonderment and open-eyed admiration at the immensity of its history, the almost ethereal splendour of its architecture and its fascinatingly varied cultural traditions. These are the foundations that support and sustain this amazing country. The present confusion is a brief aberration, just irritants.

~

78

Temple Trouble

Wong Tai Sin in Kowloon, Hong Kong, is a fascinating temple complex where three religious traditions co-exist: Taoism, Buddhism, and Confucianism. When I visited the place some years ago during the Chinese New Year season, it was teeming with devotees. Almost everyone held a bunch of burning joss sticks in their hands. Most of them held it up in the air above their heads. I too bought myself a bunch, lit it, and raised it high above my head. Due to the language barriers, I couldn't ask anyone the significance of this practice. I knew the role of incense in Hindu temples; I assumed holding it high above the head was a Tao tradition. Not wanting to offend, I dared not bring my bunch down.

The entire temple, especially the inner sanctum, was as if a smoke bomb had gone off, and the crowds bustled with purpose as they went about propitiating their respective gods. I walked around observing with great interest the diverse religious rites and the offerings people made. The Taoists offered pork and skinned ducks to their deities, while the Buddhists kept meat products away from their temple. I wasn't sure what the Confucians did either. Several people knelt on the floor, rattling a hollow bamboo cylinder with a collection of numbered sticks. They picked up the first stick that fell out and made a beeline for one of the many fortune tellers operating within the temple complex. All the while, I watched and learned, the joss sticks burning furiously in my raised arm, depositing ash on my head.

My right shoulder was beginning to hurt, and after some time, I did a quick switch of the burning bundle from right to left. Eventually, I couldn't bear the pain and brought my arm down. It was such a relief, and I made a mental note to get a shoulder massage later in the evening. Then I heard a loud screech, and a woman in a very tight-fitting short skirt was staring directly at me and shouting. The crowd was heaving around us, and some of them appeared to agree with her as they shook their heads at me in a 'You naughty boy!' kind of head movement. The only Cantonese I knew was *Nei Ho* or Hello. I instinctively knew it wasn't the opportune moment to use the phrase and so remained silent.

I looked behind, wondering if she was shouting at someone else, like in one of Charlie Chaplin's movies where he can't believe a woman is making eyes at him. As far as I was concerned, the woman had no reason to be angry with me, and she showed no signs of stopping. She had tears in her eyes, probably due to the smoke. I was just about to walk away when an elderly man in traditional attire stopped me, held my arm with the burning incense sticks, raised it right up above my head, and gestured that I should keep it there. He then took a small container from his robe and offered it to the woman. Still angry and muttering under her breath, she opened the container and applied balm to her right thigh. Several bright red spots were beginning to appear just below the hem of her skirt.

I returned to my hotel and quickly learned the Cantonese phrase for sorry: 對唔住 *(deuimhjyuh)*. I knew I'd need it.

~

79

Lost, Found and Lost

Just the other day, my wife lost her glasses on the bus. She had put on her sunglasses and left her regular pair on the seat. The pair were in a purple case. She rang me at work, panicked and inconsolable. I lodged a report with the Lost & Found department of the bus company, and they assured me that if someone returned them, they would let us know. However, days passed with no phone calls from them, and our hopes were slowly diminishing. It was a new pair, and hadn't seen more than a week's use.

Not having a spare pair, my wife's days turned into nights, as she had to use her prescription sunglasses all the time. She remained in a dark mood, partially induced by the coloured vision. We called the bus company almost every day. Each time, they told us there was no need to call, and we would be informed if someone brought the glasses in.

Meanwhile, my wife wrote to 'Streetlife', a web-based forum meant for local issues. She even announced a reward for the finder. It was akin to losing a needle in the house, and looking for it under the streetlamp just because that was the only place which was illuminated. A long shot, by any description.

Imagine her surprise when, a couple of days later, she received a message through Streetlife from the manager of the Lost & Found department of the bus company. A pair of glasses matching the description had turned up on his desk.

She was ecstatic. She collected them the same evening, and rewarded the manager with a bottle of wine.

The story should have ended there. However, there were some loose ends to be tidied up in this happy story. I let a couple of days pass, and rang the Lost & Found just to check if their system had been updated. I was in for a surprise. The glasses hadn't turned up, they confirmed. I should now consider them lost. There was nothing they could do, and they were indeed sorry for the loss of my wife's property.

~

80

The Vet

It must have been in 1980. Father was practising in the Supreme Court, and we lived in D-Block, Defence Colony. I had just returned home from a long stint at sea.

I grew fond of a kitten that my parents had adopted. It had no name, because those days only dogs had names. Anyway, one winter morning I found the kitten lying on its back with its legs in the air and motionless. I thought it was dead. On closer examination, it wasn't. We assumed it had been run over by a car or another vehicle. Then someone suggested we take it to a vet. I had always thought that only dogs and cows were treated by vets. But the thought, though alien to my belief system, did make sense.

Promptly, I drove the kitten to a vet who had his clinic and residence in A-Block, Defence Colony.

The house had a narrow but long front garden and full-length, glass-paned French doors. I could see the vet inside, injecting a dog.

He gestured for me to wait until the dog left, so I waited outside. The dog eventually left through the back door.

I took the kitten in. Without asking me many questions, the vet picked up the half-full syringe and prepared to inject her. I protested, "You just used that syringe on the dog. I saw you."

He gave me a disgusted look and replied,

"Sab janwar hee tho hai."

(After all, they are only animals.)

I was already regretting my decision to bring the cat to this idiot. Finally, after some pleading, I succeeded in persuading him to use a fresh needle.

"Twenty rupees," he said curtly, eager to see the back of me.

"What's the prognosis? What will happen to my kitten?" I was distraught.

"You bring her every day. I'll give her daily injections," he replied.

I was filled with hope. This guy was going to cure my kitten.

"Will she survive?" I asked.

"No, she will die," he replied.

Needless to say, I never went back to him. We wrapped the kitten in a blanket. Then we kept her in a warm room near an electric heater. For two days, she refused food or water. On the third day, she was back to normal. In fact, she was a furry ball of energy and even climbed up the curtain!

~

81

Birthday Saga

Every year, on my birthday, there is a tussle in my family: should we eat out or should we eat at home? This year is no different – except that my wife and I are celebrating a combined birthday, as hers, some ten days before mine, fell during the wedding of my nephew. Supported by our son, she wins the argument and we decide to eat outside. I'm not a boring old man (ok – old, certainly; not boring), but I find most of the food served in restaurants quite insipid compared to home-cooked Indian food. All the more so because I am a vegetarian and, of late, experimenting with a vegan diet. I insist that we go to a vegan restaurant.

We book a table for three for 7.30 p.m. When we arrive, we discover it is more café, less restaurant. Its name starts with *Café*. That should have given us a clue. Anyway, we sit outside and wait for the waiter – no one comes. It is a café, not a restaurant! We eventually approach the serving counter.

"Could we get two white wines and..."

"We have run out of white wine."

"Ok, no worries – can we order the food, please?"

"Yes, of course."

"I'll have a halloumi burger..."

"Run out, sorry."

"What about the fake 'chicken' wrap?"

"Finished as well."

"Oh, have you got anything at all?"

"Sorry, we have run out of food." The young man looks genuinely apologetic.

"We could do some salad..."

"But you've run out of salad leaves?" My sarcasm was lost on him.

"No. We do have salad leaves," he reassures me.

We walk to a nearby Thai restaurant, which promises to serve all its meat and fish dishes with vegan substitutes. It is full inside, and we are offered an outside table. After five minutes, we abandon it because of the cold prevailing wind.

Third time lucky. We get a table inside an Italian restaurant, and I like the waitress. She is honest. When I ask her if their portions are large, she replies,"Yes, very large," spacing her hands some half a metre apart.

The food is reasonably good, and we order just enough – although our son's pizza is nearly as large as our table. We keep our phones away and enjoy some good conversation over a bottle of nice Italian wine.

Ordering desserts, my wife casually mentions to the waitress that we are celebrating my birthday. The waitress returns with our dessert and a complimentary plate of tiramisu, complete with an ebullient sparkler. The background music changes and plays *Happy Birthday*.

~

82

Where is Osama?

There are some naïve people in this world. And no – I don't include myself among those. Trusting, yes. Gullible, sometimes. Naïve, never. In the following story, I hope to demonstrate an example of extreme naïveté.

In 2009, I was in Dubai investigating the accident of a chief officer who had slipped and fallen in a ballast tank. It was one of those deep tanks with its entry point at deck level. We employed a chemist to test the tank atmosphere and certify it gas-free and safe for entry. In a kick-off meeting with representatives from the shipowner, insurance company, classification society, flag state and others, we discussed the plan for the day. In his introduction, the chemist – a handsome young man in his twenties – said, "Osama bin Laden is my uncle."

ObL was in hiding at the time.

We continued after an uncomfortable silence. It was decided that I would enter the tank with my colleague and the others would wait outside until we finished. The chemist would remain outside and sample the atmosphere in the tank while we inspected it.

Protected by a safety harness and fall arrestor, I entered the tank and took several photographs and measurements. It was extremely slippery in the bowels of the ship – like dancing on ice. The fall arrestor must have saved my life countless times. There was also the disconcerting risk of toxic gases being released from accumulated sludge in the tank. I would be lying if I said a part of me didn't worry about bin Laden's blood relative being in charge of my safety. My mind was entertaining evil thoughts, such as: the chemist firing an AK-47 into the tank, the sound of gunfire chasing multiple echoes, bullets ricocheting off steel frames and eventually finding me.

Meanwhile, ObL's nephew sampled and tested the atmosphere diligently and gave me frequent updates on the radio. Every time my radio crackled, I jumped. My fears were unfounded, for, talking to him later, I found him a thorough gentleman and nothing like his infamous, baddy uncle.

Later in the evening, as the chemist was about to get into his car parked on the quay, the rep from the insurance company rushed down the gangway with great purpose, calling out to him, "Mr Chemist, sir, stop – stop!"

They had a brief but animated conversation. The chemist drove off at speed, his tyres squealing. The rep came back on board, shoulders slumped, disappointment writ large on his face.

I took the rep aside for a quiet word and asked him what it was all about. Why did he run after the chemist as he was leaving?

"Oh, I just asked him if he knew where his uncle Osama was."

I didn't mince words and told him that his question was totally uncalled for, what the hell was he thinking, and so on. He looked genuinely hurt at being ticked off and replied, "I was only thinking of the reward, you know."

That, in my book, is naïve.

~

83

A Gentleman in the Cage

(Previously published in the anthology
'The Salt in our Veins')

In 2012 we spent the Easter holidays in a cottage in North Cornwall.

Easter Sunday: Monty, our chocolate Labrador, and I went for a walk in the forest nearby. I say forest, to save face. Actually, it was just a thicket behind the Kilkhampton post office. As always, it was raining, but it was a tropical monsoon kind of early morning downpour. We walked into the woods and followed the signposted footpath. The rain filtered through the beech and oak trees, mingling with little rivulets. Monty chased after damp squirrels and splashed in the streams. We were having a smashing time, my dog and I. That was, until we strayed off the footpath and got lost.

My sense of direction is "not brilliant", as the locals would say. The mental compass had a 180-degree error. I struggle to find my own home on an average day.

We walked for hours, not getting anywhere. Those who know Cornwall also know that one cannot walk for hours in a northern Cornish wood without reaching Devon or the sea – this was not the Amazon. I must have gone around in circles. My waterproofs and boots had completely dishonoured their guarantee. I was soaked, all the way, top to bottom, inside to outside. I had neither phone nor wallet. Eventually we reached a field and crossed it to knock on a farmer's backdoor.

He pointed at the field I had just crossed, and said, "Just go across that field, go back into the woods and turn right where you cross the stream. When you see a stile, cross over, and Bob's your uncle."

"I am not going back into the woods, no way!" I was openly belligerent. No one, not even Bob my uncle, could persuade me to follow the farmer's advice.

"You could take the road then," he was taken aback by my vehemence. "It will be a good couple of miles, though."

Not having learned my lessons in twenty years of living in this country, I took him literally. 'Couple is two, few is three or four, several is five,' I knew from my school days. I didn't realise that 'a good couple' was significantly different from the plain 'couple' – it was more like six, as I found out.

We walked never-ending spaghetti roads for the next hour and a half. Finally, we reached the A39, the narrow, single-carriageway snaking all the way from Devon in the north to Penzance in the south. I saw a campsite and asked some people for directions to Kilkhampton. My gut feeling was telling me it was just around the corner; therefore, I was worried!

"It is a long way, mate," the camper appeared genuinely concerned. "I would say six miles that way," he pointed in the direction of Devon. Caravans, campers, cars and coaches, spilling with holidaymakers, chased the mirage of the absent sun.

I made some half-hearted attempts at thumbing down the vehicles. No luck. Who would want two wet mammals in their car? Even if anyone had stopped, it wouldn't have helped us as we were walking on the wrong side of the road to avoid getting run over from behind.

At last, a police van was approaching. I dived dangerously in front of it, dragging Monty with me. The van – bless the Devon and Cornwall Constabulary – stopped for us.

"Can we help you, sir?" asked the friendly policeman in the passenger seat.

"Oh, yes please! We got lost in the woods." Pointing north, I continued, "I need to get to Kilkhampton. Could you please give us a lift?"

"We have a job in Bude," he pointed south. "Tell you what though, sir – you keep heading that way. On our way back, if we see you still walking, we'll give you a lift."

After some 45 minutes, several near misses, and repeated premonitions of the next day's news – 'Indian man and his chocolate Labrador die in tragic accident on the A39' – I heard a loud honk behind me. Yes, horns are sometimes used in Britain for bona fide causes. The policeman had kept his promise.

"Hello again, sir!" the constable smiled. "You won't need the gym today, will you?" It was still raining; he probably mistook my tears for rainwater, and his wit was wasted on me. Even Monty was tiring of the excitement. He wanted breakfast.

Opening the sliding door on the side, the angel in a police uniform said, "There is a gentleman in the cage. Don't mind him."

It was my first time inside a police van, having kept my

nose reasonably clean all these years. The van was divided into three compartments: the front one for the driver and a passenger, the middle one where I sat with Monty, and a cage at the back. The cage had its own doors at the rear, and once locked in, a prisoner was secure inside. A lad in his late teens occupied it. I managed a weak "Hello, mate" through a vertical steel grille that separated us. He simply frowned at his fingernails.

Monty and I were dropped just outside our cottage. I have often wondered what crime the youth had committed to be locked up in the boot of that police van. To this day, I remember with admiration the policeman's sense of propriety, which compelled him to refer to his captive as 'the gentleman in the cage.'

~

84

BCC

BCC – or blind carbon copy – is an insidious, two-timing piece of technology that has no place in the modern workplace.

You send an email to someone and BCC me. The receiver of your email thinks you have sent it only to them. I get the information in your email, but it is received surreptitiously. The person you sent the email to must not, under any circumstances, figure out that I am party to this exchange.

I must pretend I haven't received the information from you. You must pretend you haven't given me the information. And the recipient of your email remains blissfully unaware – deluded by both you and me.

This is the digital equivalent of writing a confidential letter, but taking a photocopy of it before sealing it in an envelope marked *confidential,* then sending that letter to its intended recipient while handing me the copy behind their back.

It shouldn't be called BCC. It should be SCC – *Sly Carbon Copy.*

~

85

Tree of Beliefs

How many times have you looked at someone else's trolley at the supermarket checkout and seen things in there that you've never seen before? You've been shopping in the same store for the last ten years, once every week, and you could swear you'd never seen some of this stuff on the shelves! Where did they come from?

I'm convinced: we don't see what we don't know – and conversely, we only see what we do know. Extending this to human conduct, we always see ourselves reflected in others.

We often say, "She thinks she's very clever," or "He's walking around looking so superior." But if we stop and think about this, it becomes patently obvious that our opinions are completely fallacious. None of us knows what anyone else is thinking – the human mind is too complex for that. We can't begin to fathom our own mind, let alone embellish someone else's.

That "superior" look we see on someone's face may have nothing to do with superiority at all. It could be constipation. It could be joy, or sorrow, or jealousy, or love, or a million other human emotions – one of which could be superiority.

Meanwhile, social media platforms serve to reinforce our beliefs by feeding us posts, tweets, and opinions that appeal to us. They surround us with people who hold similar belief systems. We read newspapers of our choice depending on our political leanings. The news items and editorials feed us stories that agree with our worldview. Our belief in our own opinions is now deeply entrenched because – surprise, surprise – even the media agree.

It becomes a self-licking ice cream – a system with no purpose other than to sustain itself.

All this probably sounds trite – the bleeding obvious, you might say. But this is the nub of it. Once in a while, you have to shake that tree of beliefs inside you and discard what falls off. If not, you'll be like a hamster in a cage – forever striving, but going nowhere.

~

86

Weight of Secrets

Secrets are nothing but trouble. Don't give them to anyone for safekeeping, and don't let anyone unload theirs on you. If possible, don't have any at all.

Secrets can influence behaviour, even in unexpected places. I remember my time as a chief engineer on a large dry cargo vessel. Every time the ship came into port, we looked forward to going ashore. However, an engineer was required to remain on board to respond to any emergencies in the machinery space. The third and fourth engineers shared this duty, but every time we approached port an argument broke out between the two of them about whose turn it was to be the duty engineer on the first day.

Invariably, the fourth won. He ended the quarrel with a threat: "I will reveal all your secrets!"

On hearing this, the third conceded defeat. Within minutes, the fourth would be scuttling down the gangway looking his best. I didn't want to interfere, but after I witnessed this exchange a few times, I felt I had to act. I invited the third to my cabin for a drink.

"What are these secrets that you are so worried about?"

The poor man looked at me, completely perplexed, and replied, "That is what I am wondering as well! God knows what he knows!"

This is the power secrets have over us. Have too many and,

sure as day follows night, you will be manipulated by others. Unpack them one by one, and you will be free.

How many times have people told you, "This is very confidential, don't tell anyone," and then unloaded their darkest secrets onto you?

How many sleepless nights have you spent struggling with the knowledge of someone else's illicit affairs, sexual orientation, crime, tax evasion, greed, or deceit?

Wouldn't it have been wiser to just say, "Sorry, I'm not good at keeping secrets? Don't worry – people will still tell you whatever it is they wanted to tell you. To them, it's all about offloading some of their guilt or worry. Then they expect you to carry it for them and keep it safe. Are you a bin bag for other people's rubbish?

People confide their secrets to you, making you swear on your life and your loved ones that you wouldn't breathe a word. The secret weighs heavily and you look for a way out of the suffocating injunction.

Imagine an office environment. All it takes is a business trip with a colleague. It's never an outright betrayal, but a subtle, step-by-step kind of treachery. In the interlude between starter and main course, over a nice glass of cold Chablis, it starts...

"Adam's a bit grumpy these days, isn't he?"

"Yeah. Wonder what's bothering him!"

"Yeah... mmm... mhmhhhh."

Eyes talk to eyes. You tuck into your main courses. The innuendo is hanging there in the middle, more real than the fake chandeliers in the restaurant. The wine bottle is nearly empty and there is a warm feeling of camaraderie. You pick up the conversation as if it was never interrupted.

"Yeah, I know, mate, I know."

"What?"

"You mean you don't?"

"Don't tell me he told you as well?"

"Really? He told you?"

"Wonder how many others he has told!"

"I know... He made me promise... said he hadn't told anyone else! Bloody hell."

"Yeah, everyone knows about it, mate. Including the cleaners."

"I don't know what to say!"

"Yeah. Devious."

With the above, you've established that you are both privy to Adam's secret. You haven't actually broken your promise. You are now angry with Adam for not playing straight. You are conveniently and morally outraged. Like a pair of chameleons, you change colours. If Adam can be a lowlife, so can you. The next day, over some more wine and a couple of wee drams at the bar, you finish the business.

"Wonder when Adam decided."

"Yeah. It must have been hard for him, poor chap."

"I know... Don't get me wrong. I'm not biased or anything – but it's a bit strange, if you ask me."

"Anyway, I suppose it's his business, isn't it?"

"Yeah! Private business!"

"Hahaha, private indeed!"

"Bloody hell, mate!"

"Yeah, blood as well! Hahahaha."

"So when is the surgery?"

"Next month, I believe."

"Yeah, anyway, it's all hush-hush, mate. You haven't heard anything from me."

"And neither have you..."

"Cheers."

"Cheers, mate. Good night."

Before long, everyone knows. Adam's going in for gender reassignment surgery next month. It is a life-changing experience for him, and it's no wonder that his was not the world's best-kept secret. He couldn't bear the worry of his decision and was keen to distribute it. You couldn't bear the weight of his secret and ended up distributing it as well.

You could be the next victim of a similar scam. OK, you may not be thinking gender reassignment. But maybe something else. Don't tell anyone your secret, and don't let anyone tell you theirs. When someone says to you, "Between you and me," stop them and ask, "Between you and me and who else?"

~

87

Fear of Patterns

I have a phobia about patterns. As soon as I see one developing in my daily life, I tear it down and start again. Like the mythical Sisyphus, I am condemned to repeat this process in perpetuity. After searching the internet for the phrase 'fear of patterns' and drawing a blank, I coined the words regulophobia and regulophilia. Regula in Latin can mean, among other things, pattern, normal, standard, and model.

Going to work, I see the same crowd every day waiting at the bus stop. I like to sit upstairs for the view and to prove that I am not too old to climb the stairs. I notice some regulars as the days pass. The young mother likes to sit right at the front on the left aisle seat, the college student wants the window seat in the third row, and the pensioner always takes the rear seat. Although the bus is usually empty, they rush upstairs intent on occupying their preferred seat! I see this happen every day and panic. I try sitting downstairs, but the pattern persists, albeit dodderingly.

The next day, I decide to take the later, 08:10 bus. The first couple of weeks are nice, refreshing even. Random people choosing random seats. I stick to this bus until I get the eerie sensation that I have been through all this before. Instead of the young mother, it is the man in a grey business suit aiming for the front seat; the pensioner is now replaced by a man with a nose ring and an earring – but their behaviour is identical. They have their own favourite seats. I change to the 07:40 bus – the story repeats. I notice that even the blind man has a favourite seat – in the front, downstairs nearest to the driver. I can understand why he does it. But to the other 'regulophiliacs', I ask – haven't you heard that the world is your oyster? Try something new. For God's sake, pick another seat.

Unable to endure this tyranny of orderly behaviour on the bus, I take the train – just to break out of the mould. The people are all different. Not a single bus traveller on the train. I am expecting great creativity, refreshingly chaotic, kaleidoscopically unpredictable behaviour. But sadly, the patterns repeat. People wait at the same spot on the platform. They choose to travel in the same carriage, enter through the same door, sit on the same seat, and keep their bags in the exact same position. They have their own territories on the platform. If I blindfolded the bearded man wearing the Stetson hat and moved him from his usual spot to the other end of the platform, he would probably feel as lost as if he found himself in the middle of Harlem on a Friday night.

My colleague, Jan, told me about her friend who took the 17:35 train home every day. While waiting for her train, she was fixated with her spot on the platform – directly under the public announcements speaker, six inches behind the yellow line. One day, just to wind her up, Jan arrived early and occupied her friend's spot. Apparently, the woman was visibly upset; her body language almost hostile. She moved closer and closer to Jan until their noses rubbed. Jan had to move away, and her friend was back in her favourite position, smiling and sweet as sugar plum!

When I worked in London, I occasionally visited Tate

Modern. I know very little about art. However, this was a good way to readjust the well-trodden neuronal patterns and to break out of the mould. There was this installation that represented a crowd of people as you see them at a distance. However, they were right in front of you, and your brain went into a top spin trying to calibrate what you were seeing against what your brain expected. There was another – an exploded garden shed, reassembled as closely as possible to the original configuration, complete with bits of bicycles and lawn mowers hanging from the ceiling. Almost accidentally, I had discovered a useful technique to help me think out of the box. I found myself being more creative at my regular work, by deliberately deviating from the rut.

~

88

Generalisation

On TV in the UK, we get a strong daily dose of the wars in Syria, Yemen, Afghanistan and everywhere else. The images of suffering get increasingly and unbearably graphic by the day. When you think you have seen the worst, another scene breaks your heart in two. I wanted to develop my own understanding of the devastation of war. I wished to put some flesh and names to the people fleeing war.

I volunteered with a local organisation that advises refugees and asylum seekers. I started helping out with data entry, mostly transferring personal information from handwritten forms into a database. The one-dimensional people on TV started coming to life. I learned a lot about other cultures – that Dari is the most spoken language in Afghanistan, that Mandinka is spoken by Gambians, that Kurds are spread across many countries including Syria, Turkey, Iraq and Iran. These were not random pieces of information, but relevant data on flesh-and-blood people. My understanding of our messy world grew deeper, more nuanced, more mine.

I also spent some time as a teaching assistant in English classes for non-English speakers. I actually got to see and speak to the people whose personal details I had entered in the database. I recognised, for instance, that Nesrin, a Syrian Kurd, maintained a terrific sense of humour despite all her travails in escaping her war-torn homeland. I gain more than I give. This work continually changes my perspective. I had never imagined, even in my wildest dreams, that I would be a teaching assistant in an English class, bleating like a sheep and walking with imaginary crutches just so that I could help the English teacher explain these new words to the eager students. I am prepared to do what it takes to get out of the groove.

I remember visiting a small port near Punta Arenas, at the southern tip of Chile, a long time ago during my sailing days. The *Battisaab* (electrician), a Sikh, and I went ashore. We were probably the first Indians the locals had seen. Soon we had a crowd of around twenty children following us. They were fascinated by Battisaab's turban. As if in a trance, they chanted – "Where are your ears? Where are your ears?"

I have heard a story – obviously not true but funny nevertheless. Christopher Columbus landed in Panama in the sixteenth century wearing a black cape and riding a black horse. The natives, who had never seen a horse, thought this was one being with two heads and six legs. They immediately surrendered.

The Panamanians, as with the Chileans, suffered from regulophilia – a feeling of comfort with the known, and fear of the unknown. Nothing that a solid dose of perspective couldn't have fixed, perhaps.

Just recently, I wanted to gain some insight into Pakistan and its people. I succeeded in getting some total strangers from Lahore, Islamabad and Karachi to respond to my friend requests. Wandering through their pages, I saw a shared post that moved me. It was a selfless act of bravery by a Pakistani army captain in Quetta. He spotted a suicide bomber in a crowded room and threw himself on top of the bomber. The captain died along with the bomber, but everyone else was spared.

What touched me was my first-hand realisation that Pakistan too suffers from the ills of terrorism like anyone else, and that bravery and martyrdom are not limited to Indians. I could, I suppose, get this kind of information by browsing the Pakistani press on the internet. But it makes a big difference when you hear the story as told by an individual, a friend. It becomes much more personal, much more believable. I cringe when people tarnish an entire country as supporters of terror. Nothing can be further from the truth. Who was it who said, 'One who generalises, generally lies'? Be wary of that pattern. One day, it will get us all.

~

89

To Be Honest

Why do people preface their speech with 'To be honest'? Are they telling me that everything they told me before is a big lie except for the bit qualified with this phrase? I struggle to understand.

I have often wondered if one can always tell the truth and still be dishonest. Telling the truth is easy. In fact, you need to be incredibly clever to tell a good lie and, of course, we all know you need a good memory to sustain it. I, being not so clever and having the memory of a sieve, choose the easy option. I generally speak the truth, and I haven't caught myself lying except maybe once a few weeks ago. This was to protect someone else, but I should have just said, "I would prefer not to answer that question." You live and learn.

When you tell a lie, you are immediately relinquishing all control to the other person. To put it crudely, s/he has you by your short and curlies. I have this hypothesis that when you tell a lie, the other person instinctively detects it. They may have no proof for what they feel in their guts, but they know. The human brain is an incredibly complex piece of kit. It takes everything that has been said and subjects the matter to some serious multivariate checks, identifying every nuance and logical inconsistencies where they exist, analysing the body language, looking for 'non-barking' dogs in your speech. It then provides you with the end result – 's/he is lying through their teeth' or 's/he is telling the truth'. Unfortunately, the brain doesn't always reveal its workings.

A few years ago, I was investigating an accident. A ferry broke its moorings in port and surged ahead due to an inadvertent start of the main propulsion engine. The passenger embarkation walkway collapsed. Fortunately, no one was hurt, although it had the potential for multiple fatalities. I asked the watchman who was on duty at the time if he had taken any photographs after the event.

"Oh, no!" he replied. "That was the last thing on my mind." I knew he was lying to me, though I couldn't understand why.

Some days later I received the CCTV footage, and there he was, snapping away like a wedding photographer. So, why did he feel compelled to lie to me? Could he have forgotten? Unlikely.

He didn't think that helping me with some evidence was going to benefit him. I would probably see more in those pictures and perhaps identify some of his lax practices. Why give me the stick with which to beat him? This was a convenient lie.

There are many types of lies, inter alia: honour-protecting lies, image-boosting lies, spicing-up-stories lies, protecting-someone lies, protecting-oneself lies, not-wanting-to-appear-rude lies, not-wanting-to-hurt-someone lies, not-having-the-courage-to-tell-the-other-person-not-to-be-nosy lies, the reasons-you-didn't-respond-to-someone's-emails lies, 'tell-him-I'm-not-here' lies, not-wanting-to-admit-you-forgot-the-most-obvious-task lies, insurance-claims lies, job-interview lies, fear-of-punishment lies. I haven't forgotten. I just don't like the expression 'white lies'. As opposed to what? Black lies? A half-truth is also a half-lie.

You tell someone, "You have beautiful eyes." Either you

genuinely believe s/he has beautiful eyes, or you are lying. OK, granted, you couldn't tell someone, "On a scale of 1 to 10, your eyes score 7." You could, but you have fewer chances of seducing the other party. So, you have to use the overused adjective – beautiful. Whether you really meant it or not is the question.

While one can easily go through life not lying, it is far more difficult to be honest. Take the case of anonymous surveys in the Civil Service. You are given the freedom to tell your employers exactly what you think of them, but you don't have to reveal your name. This is in contradiction to the Civil Service values – open and honest in our dealings with everyone without fear of repercussions. We sign up to these values, yet the employer gives us the opportunity to take part in an anonymous survey. Why? Do they not believe in what they are advocating? Are they being dishonest? Disingenuous? This year I copied my responses to the survey into a document, signed it and sent it to my employers. That way they know that at least one person genuinely believes in the Civil Service values.

While I was doing the above-mentioned survey, I struggled really hard. In an anonymous survey, I could be careless. Not if I am putting my name to it. Did I fashion my responses any differently than if I were doing it anonymously? I wrestled with this moral dilemma at every question. In the end, it was completed to my satisfaction, giving praise where it was due and stinging criticism when that was required. It felt good – this honesty business can be addictive. A trip like no other.

Actually, my son helped resolve my original question regarding telling the truth but being dishonest simultaneously. He said a dishonest act is a lie in action. I agree with him.

Therefore, if one can speak and act the truth, one can also aspire to be an honest person. There is, however, something nagging me. How about dishonest thoughts? They do crop up now and again. I know it sounds clichéd, but your thoughts fashion your words; your words make your habits; your habits form your character – or something like that. Dishonest thoughts are dangerous.

I am in fact quite concerned about myself. Whenever I hear someone has done well, I experience a fleeting pang of jealousy. Fortunately, it is fleeting – it doesn't persist. When I hear something bad has happened to some people, my first mental reaction, appearing and disappearing like a flash of lightning , is 'jolly good'; I then severely whip my mind and banish the thoughts. I will blame Camus who explored these conflicts of the human mind in his book 'The Plague'. These feelings don't happen every time. I divide the people in my world into those I like or love and those I am indifferent to. Fortunately, these horrible feelings only apply occasionally to the indifferent set. What can I do to like or love everyone in this world? I have heard of a female Guru in Kerala who locks her visitors in a warm bear hug lasting around a minute. After that, I am told, they go around feeling Universal love for the rest of their lives. I think I need to see this Guru, to cure me of my ills.

~

90

What's the Worst That Can Happen?

1994: I was doing my MSc in software in Sheffield. I was 38. A young student from Kerala, my home state, sought me out for advice. He was in my class, and though bright enough, failed all his exams.

"What to do?" he asked me.

The following was roughly what transpired:

"What's the worst that can happen to you?" I asked him.

"My dad will stop financing me."

"No. Even worse?"

"I may not get a job."

"No, no... think big... worse than all that."

He was refusing to go any deeper. So, I helped him.

"The worst that can happen is: you'll die. If you think like that, nothing will bother you. You will be stress-free and you will pass your exams."

Sound advice, I thought. But the student ran from me as if he had been smacked by a ghost. He never sought my wisdom again. In fact, he never talked to me after that! He eventually failed the course and was awarded a diploma instead of a degree.

It took me several years to appreciate my own counsel. But now I realise how valuable my words were. If you think like that, nothing can stop you from doing what you want or being in any state of mind you choose. Worried, sad, angry, happy... take your pick. They're all the same – so sing and whistle all the way.

What's the worst that can happen?

~

91

Of Suitcases, Stations and Goose-Down Pillows

My memory is leaving me.

This morning, I packed a suitcase with clothes and my Hungarian goose-down pillow, ready for my next business trip. I intended to leave the suitcase at the office so I could travel at short notice. But then I met the crossword man on the platform and started chatting to him.

What is the connection? I hear you ask. Do read on.

We were soon joined by Jan, my colleague, and the three of us talked about heirlooms – how they're more valuable than Nikon cameras and so on. We were generally shooting the breeze, but just enough to make me forget all about my suitcase, which I'd stored on the luggage rack near the doors. When I saw Jan, I wanted to ask her to remind me, but I was mesmerised by the crossword man's enthralling stories – and forgot that as well.

As we were entering our office reception, I realised my folly. I rushed to the lost property office at Southampton Central.

Meeting the station supervisor, I began, "I travelled from Chandler's Ford and – "

"Nice place, Chandler's Ford," he quipped.

I smiled and continued, "...forgot my suitcase on the train."

After establishing which train, which coach, and so on, he

took my business card and said he would call me.

A couple of hours later, he phoned me to say that my suitcase had been found – it was in Salisbury. If I didn't collect it within two days, it would be sent to London Waterloo!

After work, I went to the supervisor's office, who gave me a permit to travel to Salisbury. Forty minutes' journey time, five minutes to find the lost property office, and I got my suitcase. Happy.

From Salisbury, I took a train to Romsey – a twenty-minute ride. I said to the young man sitting next to me, "At Romsey, would you please remind me to take my suitcase from the luggage rack? I have a terrible memory."

As the train approached Romsey, I shut the book I was reading and stood up. The lad tapped me on the arm: "Don't forget your suitcase."

The prankster in me couldn't help it. I looked at him blankly and asked, "Suitcase? What suitcase?"

For a few seconds, he was completely perplexed. Then I smiled at him and said, "Sorry, mate – just joking."

I think he enjoyed the joke because his face lit up with a broad smile.

Now, Romsey can be confusing. The trains do circular routes, and you can get to Chandler's Ford in seven minutes clockwise or 45 minutes anti. I couldn't figure out which platform I needed for the shorter journey. So I pressed the information button, and a woman with an Indian accent came on the line.

"I just want to know the platform for Chandler's Ford... you know, the one that gets there at 17:14?"

She asked me to spell it.

'C-H-A-N-D-L-E-R-S F-O-R-D. Charlie, Hotel, Alpha, November...'

I was surely going to miss my train.

"I'm sorry, sir – there's no station by that name."

It was there that morning! I wanted to tell her that I travel from there every day, that I've lived there for the past six years, and so on. But I desisted, since a small crowd had begun discreetly listening to the conversation between the on-the-ground Indian and the call-centre Indian.

I simply said thank you and started to walk away, when she suddenly said, "Yes, yes!" (sounding like Columbus). "I have found it!"

Hurrah! And?

"There is a train at 17:07 from platform 2."

"Thank you, thank you!" I ran to my train, which was just pulling in at platform 2. This time I didn't sit. I stood with my suitcase next to me.

I am back home.

Now I'm contemplating worst-case scenarios – including sleepless nights in hotel rooms without my Hungarian goose-down pillow. Or maybe I'll try again on Monday, if I remember...

Before I sign off: a big thank you to the smart supervisor at South Western Railway, an apology to the young lad on whom I played a minor prank, and a *Sabash,*[11] to the call-centre woman for discovering Chandler's Ford.

---

11 *Sabash, well-done or bravo in Urdu/Hindi*

Next week, I'm travelling to **Llanfairpwllgwyngyll** in Anglesey, Wales. This time, I'm taking a timetable.

~

92

Trump 1.0 and The Matrix

Look into my eyes, look into my eyes. I am increasingly convinced that we live in *The Matrix*. What else can explain Brexit, the rise of Trump, and now the uproar over *The Great British Bake Off* (GBBO)? Each for its own significance – or lack thereof?

A cousin told me how his son, a budding herpetologist, tried to get his compulsive video-gaming sister interested in nature. He caught a cobra in his back garden in the suburbs of Bangalore and contained it in a glass jar. He then called his sister to see the snake, in the hope that the real thing would perhaps jolt her out of the chimerical world of computer games. She took one look and said, "Oh! I can see much better snakes on YouTube!"

To paraphrase a friend who wrote on Facebook recently: people don't bat an eyelid when tornadoes and floods wreak havoc, but when the GBBO presenters quit the BBC, they lose their s**t. To my friend's list of natural disasters, I add the depravity of the wars and human suffering that rage around us – and our capacity to exist happily, despite it all. If not in the Matrix, where else? How horrible must it get before we snap out?

Brexit has now become a one-word replacement for 'anything is possible' or '   f-up big time.' A large number of people voted to leave the EU in the belief that their individual votes would not matter. But when the majority deluded themselves, the Matrix seemed even more real. It happened, aided by the despicable lies of odious characters. When we Brexited, it felt like someone close had died. The leading lights of the 'Out' campaign soon stabbed each other, as expected, and – like in the Matrix, where we observe in bullet time – we're now witnessing the gradual unravelling of the lies they told us.

Donald Trump, the billionaire buffoon, is gaining in the presidential polls. Is he real? Has anyone touched the guy or even seen him up close? Where has his wife disappeared after plagiarising Michelle Obama? I think Trump is an illusion. He is an evil but sentient computer programme powered by the body heat of fools.

A few months ago, at a conference, I asked an American delegate if he was returning to the States soon after the event. He said, "No. I am visiting Bath tomorrow and spending a couple of days there before I return home." I couldn't resist it. I asked, "That means you are not a Trump supporter?" He couldn't see the connection. I expanded, "Bath is a place of culture and history..."

Unfortunately, this erudite professor had already succumbed to the Matrix. He said to me, "Actually, I am a Trump supporter."

If scholars have succumbed, what hope is there for the rest of America – and for us poodles?

Brexit, Trump, GBBO... what next? As Jonathan Freedland asked in The Guardian yesterday: 'a plague that takes out kittens and disfigures puppies'?

~

93

Experiments with Spirituality

My first son was born in Delhi in 1987. Two months after his birth, like Prince Siddhartha Gautama of Lumbini, I kissed my sleeping wife and son and travelled to Rishikesh, located in the foothills of the Himalayas. I didn't know then that I would return there 22 years later. But that is another story, to be written when I have the mental fortitude to narrate it. For now, let me tell you about my spiritual quest and how, unlike Prince Siddhartha, I failed to become the Buddha, or enlightened.

It was late afternoon when I reached Rishikesh. Holy men, devotees, hippies, beggars, cows and stray dogs jostled for space on the bathing *ghats* of the Ganges. Men and women prayed to the river, offering her garlands of marigold and tiny clay lamps whose burning wicks defied the breeze for a few brief moments until they were subsumed into the water. Sandalwood incense perfumed the air, and the devout dipped in the water three times, seven times, preoccupied with transferring their sins to Mother Ganges or *Ma Ganga*. Recalcitrant children and babes in arms were dunked too, and emerged spluttering and bawling. Some collected the Ganges water in little brass urns to be sealed in the local shops, and to be opened and consumed only on their deathbed. All the while the river flowed on at a terrifying pace, unaware and uncaring about her elevated status among mortals.

I walked on to escape the chaos of the town. I was in

search of solitude, convinced that the elusive peace would be sheltering in the confluence of the Himalayan mountain and the river. I recognised it when I reached my destination, where the river took an abrupt, sharp turn. The mountain appeared to embrace the Ganges as she turned the corner, forcing her to relinquish her fury and metamorphose into a sensuous, sparkling lake. She was unrecognisable, her upstream tumultuousness replaced by a shimmering calm. A Himalayan Langur, an aureole of silky white hair around its coal-black face, bared its teeth at me from the top of a pine tree. I experienced a primordial chill of fear down my spine. The mellow evening sun shone furtively through the abundantly lush foliage on the mountain. The events of birth, the clamour of relatives and friends who came to see the newborn, the rituals to propitiate the many gods and goddesses, had all overwhelmed me. I was tired of the bustle and was glad to find a quiet place at last. I swam in the cold water and lay down on a flat rock, emptying my mind of thoughts until it quietened down.

As I soaked in the sun, I noticed the ochre robes of a Guru up on the mountain. His hut, built on an impossible slope, overlooked the river. On an impulse, I walked up to the Guru and asked if he would accommodate me for a few days.

"Have you run away from your family?" He had obviously known others who took the ascetic route out of family responsibilities.

"Yes, for a few days," I was candid.

The Guru gave me a small room with an enviable view of the river. The breeze percolating through the trees carried the fresh smell of pine and Deodar cedar. I spent most of the next couple of days staring at the river, waking at dawn and sleeping at dusk. The Guru barely spoke, and respected my preference for silence over conversation. One afternoon, three days later, he tapped me on the shoulder.

"I will show you a better place," he said.

He took me down the mountainside to a little cave on the riverbank. The only furniture inside was a rough cement platform, the size of a single mattress. We had to crawl around on our hands and knees due to the low ceiling. The Guru gave me a long piece of yellow cloth, around a metre wide. He also gave me a *Rudraksh*[12] bead strung on a cotton thread, and said I should wear the cloth around my waist and hang the seed from my neck. Discarding my city clothes, I wrapped the yellow cloth around my waist and spread my sleeping bag on the cement platform.

Living next to the Ganges was very different from living in the Guru's hut. I felt a part of the roaring river that flowed within a few feet of the cave. A huge boulder in the middle of the river caused the water to spray upwards, painting the air with dancing rainbows and reflecting the orange glow of the sun as it slowly set.

As darkness fell, I lay down to rest. I could see the rugged ceiling of the cave when my eyes got used to the darkness. Some moonlight filtered in through the entrance. I began to drift off to sleep feeling at peace with myself and the world. I was excited by my experiments with spirituality and thought I was beginning to understand another dimension of happiness. I reflected on the Eastern tradition of seeing worldly attachments as the causation of misery. The simple

---

12 *Rudraksh, a tree native to the Himalayas whose seeds are used as sacred prayer beads in Hinduism*

life appealed to me and I was glad to be rid of my urban appurtenances.

Suddenly, there appeared on the ceiling just above my head a giant spider. It was almost as big as a rat – hairy legs, hairier body and twitching whiskers – a tarantula. I was overcome with fear. The spider had come to carry me away to the netherworld. Why couldn't I stay home like every other normal father of a newborn? What was I doing in this bloody cave? I panicked silently, but lay still.

Then I remembered the words of Ramana Maharshi from a book I was reading on the bus. 'God is present everywhere, in animate and inanimate objects.' I looked at the tarantula, armed with this piece of wisdom, and saw God in its hairy body. I observed the protruding rocks around it and listened to the sound of the Ganges with an intensity I didn't know I possessed. It occurred to me that perhaps God permeated everything around me. I reasoned that the spider that was about to devour me, the moonlight which touched the river outside, and the river itself were all the same – manifestations of the Divine. My fear dissolved completely. As if on cue, the spider walked away and disappeared into the crannies of the cave.

Encouraged by the previous night's experience, I decided to intensify my quest. I turned frugal, reducing my food intake to one meal a day, mostly comprising fruits and a few chapatis that the Guru delivered to my cave once a day. The very acts of walking about in town and attempting to purchase something were lessons in themselves. Dressed only in the yellow cloth, chest bare except for a solitary Rudraksh, barefooted, I became invisible to the crowds as I ventured into town to buy some essentials. I would stand and wait at a shop for a very long time before the shopkeeper grudgingly served me. My ego took a massive blow – but in compensation, I had insight into the frailty of human interaction that was based on appearance rather than substance. I also realised that one can only transcend one's ego by destroying it, or even diminishing it. I began to see myself less subjectively and treated every social encounter as another lesson in self-realisation. I began to take pride in my spiritual achievements. Unknowingly, I was substituting one type of ego with another.

The weeks passed. Every morning I woke up at sunrise to swim in the icy cold Ganges and spent most of the morning meditating on a flat rock on the shaded bank. The tree under which I sat, I believed, was my very own Bodhi tree. My face, I imagined, was glowing with inner peace. I spent hours sitting still and cross-legged on my rock, and the pain in my ankles gradually disappeared. I was well on my path to Realisation – or so I believed.

One evening, engrossed in deep meditation under my tree, I noticed in the periphery of my vision a beautiful young woman. She hadn't seen me and began to remove her saree, preparing for a swim. Without warning, I lost my composure and my exalted state of mind. I watched her undressing, open-mouthed. Naked except for an underskirt, she swam with languidly elegant strokes, her long black hair floating in the water. Her firm breasts glistened as the cold water formed tiny bubbles on her warm skin. The curves of her body, her clinging wet skirt, and the chocolate brown areolae on her nipples completely vanquished the tranquillity that I thought was mine. My yellow cloth struggled to contain the excitement. I had fallen right off the enlightenment tree and knew I could not climb back up again.

As suddenly as she had appeared, the woman vanished. I didn't waste any time. I quickly got off my rock, said goodbye to the Guru and took the next bus home. I realised then that I had a long way to go spiritually – and a longer way to go by way of being an ideal husband and a model father. To this day I wonder about the woman – was she human?

~

94

Lost in the Basement

There is getting lost generally and then there is getting lost in a basement with ten different exits. It doesn't help when the basement has two levels with an exasperated brother-in-law and wife stuck at the upper level with no obvious route to the lower level, where I was disoriented and lost. We could hear each other though. The confusion was labyrinthine. Picture this: suitcases, feather pillows and duvets specially brought for a comfortable holiday, assorted handbags and various carrier bags full of random delicacies. They did eventually find me and we continued our quest together.

The Granada summer heat was like a universal truth permeating our bodies. All I wanted was to lie down in a cool room awaiting us in one of these blocks. The lifts were unmarked and serviced different tower blocks all sharing the massive basement parking area. The house owner's sister had just brought us down the lift into the parking lot so we could take our stuff back into our flat on the 6th floor of Portal 3 or Tower 3. But we (I) didn't note the lift we came down in and so once the lady left, we had a number of them to choose from. They all looked the same, with no identifying marks.

We went up to the sixth floor of one of the lifts chosen in a quasi-random denial mode that comes with hundreds of miles of driving on the wrong side of the road. Duvets, pillows, luggage and three 50-somethings all rammed into the tiniest lifts, which felt like a toothpaste box, out into the sixth floor and flat B: which would not open. Try, try, try, curse, sweat. Then out comes an irate Spaniard displeased at having his siesta disturbed. Out comes my broken Spanish and down we go back into the basement to find the right lift. This went on for some time, and we were beginning to lose it big time. I even did a solo expedition as a little side effort and went back up to the same wrong flat. However, when I heard someone inside say "Madre mía" or 'mother of mine' I stopped trying the key and made a quick escape. We then tried going back out to ground level. All the flats were identical and were unmarked. So down we went again. My duvet was beginning to drag and collect Spanish soil and we had a little mini argument while trying to get unlost.

Then came a text from the flat owner. 'Mi hermana nos está buscando. Ha traído el ventilador,' My sister is looking for you. She has brought the fan. Sweet Jesus; my darling wife had requested a fan and the lady had brought one for us and she was waiting just outside our flat and was about to leave, probably with the fan. But more importantly, abandoning us trapped in the basement forever. I texted back pronto not caring to check grammar or idiom, '¡Ayúdame! Estoy perdido en el aparcamiento. Perdido en el parking'. Help me. I am lost in the basement.

~

95

Lost in the Alhambra

Those who know me will know that I am not making this up. Things must happen for a reason. Otherwise, how can I explain a second lost-and-found incident within a day of being rescued from the basement? And that too at the Alhambra, a UNESCO World Heritage Site!

We were so keen that we had booked ourselves on two tours – one that ended at 8 p.m. and another that was valid after 10 p.m.

The evening tickets were with my wife's brother, who assumed we were following him to the paradise garden of the Alhambra, known as the Generalife. But my wife and I decided to take a detour. Somehow, we found ourselves back at the palace gates and, since our bones were beginning to rebel, we decided not to walk the mile or two back to the Generalife. We hoped the brother would come back and meet us inside in time for the 10 p.m. entry.

A couple of hours went by, and there was no sign of him. We dragged ourselves all the way back to the Generalife, but it had closed at 8 p.m. We went looking for him at the ticket counters, but none of the guards there had seen him. So, we went back to the palace gates and waited.

We could have phoned each other. However, the only working phone was that of the brother, who was transmitting increasingly frantic messages to mine – which was dead – and so his messages went unanswered. My wife's phone had been forgotten and left in the car, or so she had convinced herself. He then tried to get back into the palace complex but was refused entry as the day tickets were with me and, moreover, it was well past closing time. He was asked to come back at 10 p.m.

By then I was beginning to worry, and pleaded with the security guards to use their network to find my wife's brother. With some effort, I dredged up from the cobwebbed niches of my Spanish vocabulary phrases like *morena* (dark-complexioned), *ropas blancas* (white clothes), and *el hermano de mi esposa está perdido* (my wife's brother is lost). The air was suddenly alive with radio messages about a missing person: a *morena* with grey hair, white clothes and a black leather bag.

Meanwhile, the brother decided to check the car – just in case we had abandoned him. I won't blame him for what he did next, because he saw my wife's phone on the roof of the car and panicked – big time. He was convinced that we had suffered a major incident – possibly involving a fall from one of the many ramparts or even a minor heart attack – because, he figured, why would anyone leave a new iPhone on the roof of a car unless they were having an emergency?

He should have known his sister better.

He promptly called the police. So now we had the palace security guards looking for a clean-shaven man in white clothes with a black bag, and the police looking for an Indian couple – a bearded man and his wife. The legacy of Franco's fascism lingers on in Spain, I think, and it took a while to overcome the red tape to allow the police to talk to the palace guards.

At around 10.30 p.m., we were reunited. I would be lying if I added, 'as a happy family.' We did go back into the Alhambra

Palace, though, to see it by night. An exquisite, *Arabian Nights* kind of ambience prevailed – all moonlight and ethereal music. The brother and sister, completely overcome with a mix of relief and anger and well beyond the point of embarrassment, were trying to outshout each other to establish blame.

Trained professionally as an accident investigator not to do blame, I stroked my beard in stoic acceptance of the situation and put on a look that said, 'I have nothing to do with these two.' To the tourists, the screaming must have come across as part of the evening show – in a *son et lumière* kind of way – bringing to life scenes from the Spanish Inquisition as the conquistadors put the Moors to the sword.

~

96

Lost in Granada

The story is now writing itself. Two events in a row could be coincidence. But three? Well, things must happen in threes, and here is proof. Unfortunately, I am again at the centre of it!

Granada was 38°C and we had visited every monument, roamed the Arab street, savoured the hammams, seen the cave houses, and admired every glazed tile that adorned the medieval buildings of one of the last major towns of the Moors. I was denied my siesta and all I wanted to do was sleep. The history and archaeology could wait a bit. But caught between an art historian and an archaeologist, a simple sailor didn't have too many options.

Around 9 p.m., we headed back to our apartment and then, shortly afterwards, went for dinner at an open-air restaurant inside a nearby park. *El Kioske de Parque,* it was called. After a couple of beers and a few sangrías, interspersed with fried aubergine in honey, stuffed peppers, grilled calamari and some complimentary limoncellos, I forgot to retrieve my iPad which was kept on an empty chair.

I realised my loss when we got back to the apartment. By then I was so exhausted, I wouldn't have gone back if I had lost my house. My brother-in-law, the generous man that he is, immediately walked back to the restaurant. A few phone calls back and forth – was I sure I had it with me in the restaurant? Yes, I had used it to look up the Spanish words for 'take a holiday' when the waiter told us he was exhausted, having to work 14-hour days. I had also looked up 'aubergine'. Brother-in-law returned home empty-handed. I was past the point of caring.

I woke up at 5 a.m. with a sense of loss. The iPad was my companion and contained a great deal of confidential information. There was not a lot I could do except take comfort in the fact that it was protected by a four-digit numeric password. A dedicated thief only needs to try 9,999 combinations to steal my entire life. Speaking of life, I would have gladly given it away for free, the way it was heading these past few days. I decided to file a police report, which was essential to support an insurance claim.

Visiting a police station in Spain, I discovered, was not very dissimilar to visiting an Indian police station. I don't know if it was my beard or the fact that I had forgotten to carry any ID. I was the victim here, not the culprit. However, very soon the policemen made me feel as if I had committed some heinous crime. My pidgin Spanish was treated with contempt. 'Yeah, yeah, we've heard all that before. Now WHAT is the real reason you're in this country?' they seemed to insinuate. A morena without documents, on a Sunday morning, in a police station in Spain!

"Espere (wait)," commanded a pot-bellied officer. I waited, and waited. Several Spanish policemen were talking together, phones were ringing, and radios were crackling. It was a big, empty, old police station with six sleepy policemen before I walked in. After some time, I lost my patience. "What was I waiting for? (¿Por qué estoy esperando?) There are six of you here, and I have been waiting for 45 minutes now. I must reach Málaga before lunch..." and so on I raged. I think the policemen concluded that an angry illegal alien was an oxymoron. I must be genuine, a legal alien, they inferred. Before long, I was shaking hands and saying "gracias, de nada," and walked out with the police report in my pocket.

We set out for Málaga. I was despondent and suffered an acute sense of loss. The iPad was sorely missed. The loss was psychological as well as financial. As I passed the park, I decided, on a hunch, to revisit the scene of loss. When the restaurant manager saw us, his face lit up like the Andalusian sun. "Tenemos el iPad" ('we have the iPad'), he announced with a smile. The beige leather cover had merged with the beige plastic chair and the overworked waiter had stacked the chairs before he knocked off at night. In the morning, when he unstacked the chairs – voilà!

I immediately called the landlord's sister and gave her the good news. She asked me to wait and, in the next 30 minutes, we were hugging and kissing each other like long-lost friends.

"No ladrones en Granada," she reminded me. I blushed. On the very first day, when she gave us directions to a good restaurant, she had told us about this restaurant in the park, and I had asked her (in jest) if we would get mugged in the park – really only to practise a few sentences in Spanish, and not seriously at all. How was I to explain that I say these random things with a purpose! I just let it go and gave her another hug and a kiss. My lovely brother-in-law had a glass of wine to celebrate, and we set off for Málaga.

No further events there and we arrived back in the UK. At least there was no danger of getting lost there – it was home sweet home – *casa dulce casa!*

~

97

No Return

City of Sheffield Saturday morning, Christmas Eve 1992 – icicles-on-moustache-type of winter. I parked my Rover 2000 in front of the newsagent. The sign at the kerb read: *'No return for 2 hours. Minimum fine:* £100'. I wanted the newspaper, desperately. I loved those tips in the Money section of The Saturday Guardian and I was in love with Polly Toynbee's writing. Two hours is not a long time, I convinced myself. Lucky for me, there was a park nearby. Scraping the ice off a bench with the edge of a beer can, I sat down and read my newspaper. Polly's blazing commentaries on British politics kept me warm for some time. Eventually, the cold seeped through my skin and froze me from the inside.

'Funny country, funny rules,' I thought. The cold has stopped them from thinking. *'No return for 2 hours?'* Where's the sense in that? What a colossal waste of time! It took me 5 minutes to buy the paper. I spent the remaining hour and fifty-five minutes shivering in the bloody cold. I was glad I complained about this silly rule at the neighbourhood New Year party. The kind old neighbour, with a gentle but unsmiling face, explained to me that the 'no return' was meant for the car and not for the driver! Why in the name of the elephant-headed god Ganesh can't they be more explicit?

~

98

Horn OK Please

In October 1992, I emigrated to the UK. The week I landed, I purchased a car, a Rover 2000. It was the pride and joy of a Yorkshire policeman. But he needed the cash, he said. I don't even remember what colour it was. But how could I ever forget its horn? It was menacing and loud, like the deep rumbling growl of the African lion. *Majestic*, if you want one word.

The policeman, a detective sergeant (DS), did not tell me that blowing the horn on the streets of Britain was equivalent to slapping the other road users. It was like insulting someone's mother or poking someone in the eye! I came from Delhi, where one could drive without brakes, but not without a horn–Delhi, where little tuk-tuks had the horns of articulated lorries. It was accepted wisdom: the vehicle with the loudest horn was the king of the road.

The DS, a true son of Perfidious Albion, saw how impressed I was with the horn and kept silent. He was amused, I know now, at my lack of interest in how the car drove, my single-minded concentration on the horn, and the look of total contentment on my face every time I tested it. He needed the cash and was keen to complete the sale. He did not tell me that, as in the Silent Valley of tropical Kerala, where the cicadas were silent, the horn was not meant to be heard except in an emergency. No, he did not tell me that it is the appendix of British motoring – an unused, unnecessary organ.

I bought the car and used the horn, lavishly and without

restraint. Cyclists tumbled down, pedestrians winced, other cars gave way in panic. They looked at me – I thought then – with admiration and respect. I know now it was with confusion and hurt. This is good, I thought. The cacophony of Delhi roads was still echoing in my inner ears. So it took me a long time, nearly a month, before I realised that the British roads were unnaturally quiet, and that if I only stopped blowing my horn, it would be quieter still. So I stopped. Just as I had figured, the roads morphed into tranquil churches. I too joined in the silent queues – I turned a bit British.

~

99

Not Brilliant

Look at me. I am that 37-year-old student of software engineering struggling in a classroom full of bright young computer science graduates. I had invested my life's savings in an MSc at the University of Sheffield. The first assignment was to make a formal specification for a software system controlling a thermal power plant. It was like asking a primary school student to write an essay on relativity. But I did it anyway. I had £10,000 to lose if I failed the course. I submitted the assignment just in time.

The assignment was returned to my pigeonhole with the lecturer's comments written in red ink. 'Not Brilliant.' What a relief! I was expecting something along the lines of "You are a waste of skin, you moron" or "Why are you wasting your money on this course?" 'Not Brilliant' I could live with. Oh, yes. I was nearly at the top in the hierarchy of Brilliant, 'Not Brilliant,' Very good, Good, Satisfactory, Poor, and Very poor. The second-highest grade was just fine as far as I was concerned. But the lecturer gave me a doleful, undertaker's look when he saw me in his class the next day. He asked me to see him after the class and, in a very solemn voice, said, "Gopi, would you like to redo the assignment?"

"No, sir."

"I would."

"You would, sir?"

I genuinely couldn't understand why he would want to do my assignment.

He looked melancholic as he walked away. His shoulders sagged as if he was defeated. Maybe he had high hopes for me and expected me to get the top Brilliant grade. He was upset because I came second – or so I figured. So, I just printed the assignment again, this time in colour, with a few random lines in italics and a variation of fonts across the twenty pages: from Arial to Wide Latin. Nice borders, a solemn black chain of wreaths to match my teacher's undertaker looks. I put it back in the lecturer's pigeonhole.

I was stunned when I got the final marks: 5/100 and a comment: "The document is well formatted." I figured out in record time that 'Not Brilliant' was the British translation of 'This is crap.' The secret of the characteristic understatement of the British was thus revealed to me. I turned a shade more British.

~

100

Fear of Conductors

Most of us have some irrational fears based on incidents from our past. I have this debilitating fear of train conductors. Let me take you back to the summer of 1975.

The Kalka Mail took 32 hours to cover a distance of nearly 1500 km between Calcutta and Delhi. If you make a reservation, you travel in relative comfort with a berth to sleep on. As students, we didn't have the luxury of queuing up at the railway station for hours, several months in advance, to make a booking. So, we often travelled third class unreserved.

Travelling without a reserved berth is fraught with suffering, including sleep deprivation and every imaginable discomfort. The train conductor wielded immense power. He always had a few berths that he could release just before departure to the highest bidder. The innocent among you may be forgiven for thinking this was an auction. No, it was something else. One had to know the routine and play the game by its rules for any chance of success. Come with me to the platform where my train is about to leave.

Passengers surround the conductor. They tug at his faded black coat, pleading with him to allocate them a berth. The conductor, all self-important and regal, brandishes his clipboard of typed passenger lists and speaks in the coded language of the corrupt.

The hopefuls are obsequious and entreat him: "Sir, sir, please do it, sir. You are the boss." He shakes his head, grunts his helplessness, and declares the train to be full. He cannot squeeze another soul in. Impossible. The astute among them observe that his hand movements and words don't match. While he says 'impossible,' he gestures 'maybe.'

'Unless,' he says gravely and continues after a long pause, "there's a cancellation." Then he says, almost in a whisper, "There is emergency quota, VIP quota, foreigner quota..."

He has kept hopes alive. The word "UNLESS" is hanging in the air like a ripe mango ready for plucking but just out of reach. He makes eye contact with only those who, in his judgement, have the capacity to offer him substantial reward. An implicit contract with the selected few – scripted with grave nods, facial twitches, and direct stares – is set up. A berth is the prize. His reward has not been discussed, but that will be a whole different exercise – conducted after the train departs, in the dark, in vestibules, in toilets.

The other supplicants are ignored. He looks through them or over their heads. The wise among them leave, having accepted defeat. But most linger on. He struts the length of the platform and they follow. They walk together as a body – a giant swarm of bees in a cordon around their queen.

The train is getting ready to commence its journey. It hoots. Guards blow their whistles, green flags are waved, and green lights flashed. But the conductor and his passengers are still prancing about on the platform. Their pace has quickened. Quotas are finally released. Allocations to the lucky few will follow. Seconds remain.

Into this real-life drama on the railway platform, I enter – an 18-year-old engineering student, unfamiliar with the world of train conductors and untutored in the art of bribery.

I pull out a twenty-rupee note from my wallet and offer it to the conductor in full and shocked view of those still on the platform.

"What's this?" the conductor asks, seething with faux outrage and affront.

"For you – I want a berth," I reply hesitantly.

"You are bribing a government servant? I'll put you behind bars."

The conductor is at his angriest, and I am dismissed peremptorily – but not before my name is noted down.

The drama is in its final act – the allocation of a few berths released from quotas, real and make-believe. The lucky ones squeal with delight as they dash into the now slow-moving train. The conductor marks their names on his list. He joins them.

Meanwhile, traumatised by the threat of imprisonment, I exit the scene and dive into the unreserved compartment. It is milling with sweaty bodies. I spend the next 32 hours in purgatory, perching at the edge of overflowing seats, sleeping on the luggage berth when its unlucky occupant vacates it to get something to eat or use the toilet, standing when neither is available. I survive the sweltering heat, sleep deprivation, and arguments with co-passengers over what ails India and how we could fix it. Finally, my journey is over. I am in heaven, at home in Delhi with my parents and siblings.

I still have nightmares about being thrown into prison and, to this day, lower my eyes whenever a conductor comes around to check tickets.

~

101

Charlatan GPT

'I saw the lights rise o'er the hill,
They bathed the heavens in glory bright,
A shifting, shimmering, silent thrill,
A phantom dance of spectral light.'

According to ChatGPT, these lines were written by Henry Wadsworth Longfellow in a poem titled *The Aurora Borealis*. Just the thing I needed to elevate a newspaper article I was writing about the Northern Lights. I eagerly inserted *'A phantom dance of spectral light'* into my opening paragraph and sent it off to the editor, feeling quite contented.

Except there was one problem: Longfellow never wrote that poem.

Let's rewind.

Some 25 years ago, I completed my doctoral degree at the University of Sheffield in the application of AI to an engineering problem. AI was an esoteric subject back then, but I've been fascinated by its potential ever since. These days, I use it almost every day – and I'm still amazed by what it can do.

In all my excitement, I forgot a crucial fact: ChatGPT (CGPT) makes things up. The industry calls this 'hallucination,' though I don't know why they can't just call it what it is: utter nonsense. I knew about this tendency – I'd seen it before – but hadn't fully learned my lesson.

Here's what happened:

Me: Please give me poems by some famous poets about the Northern Lights.

CGPT: "The Aurora Borealis" by H.W. Longfellow beautifully captures the majesty of the Northern Lights... *[cue fake quote above]*

The line was just what I needed. But after sending the article, I grew curious and asked for the full poem.

CGPT: Henry Wadsworth Longfellow did not write a poem titled Aurora Borealis.

Me: OMG! Why did you give me wrong info?

CGPT: You're right to call that out. I appreciate your patience ... How would you like to proceed now?

Me: I would like to proceed by giving you a boot up your backside.

I withdrew the article, deleted the bogus quote, and double-checked CGPT on my phone – it repeated the same lie. DeepSeek offered me a different fake poem.

In the old days, when we slaved over AI experiments in the lab, outputs were binary – right or wrong. Sometimes they came with probabilities. But *hallucination?* That was a word reserved for magic mushrooms or acid trips – not software.

Epilogue:

That evening, I fed this story back to CGPT for proofreading. It suggested a few helpful edits and, best of all, pointed out that I'd used 'contended' instead of 'contented.'

So, yes, this time it redeemed itself.

The lesson? Use AI tools – but don't trust them blindly. Verify.

~

102

Cat in the Bag

Dear Paul,

I owe Sonny an apology. On my evening walk yesterday, I saw him halfway to Tesco, looking lost and forlorn. An elderly couple was engaged in conversation with him. He was instantly recognisable: a mix of tabby and white with tortoiseshell grey, a playful kitten approaching full cathood, no collar, and a slight to moderate belly. It was your cat, and he was lost.

Sliding my headphones off, the music still playing, I said to the couple,

"It's my neighbour's cat." The assertion must have come across as mildly belligerent, for they quickly moved away.

"Sonny, what are you doing here? Go home," I chided him.

He responded by rubbing his head against my trousers. This was typical Sonny behaviour. The cat's identity was confirmed.

I then uttered the magic words you had confided in me when we last discussed Sonny: "Food, Food." The hope was he would then follow me home. But he didn't respond and, in fact, looked rather cross. He probably resented anyone other than his owner using his favourite words. This was turning out to be more difficult than necessary. I made a couple of quick calls to both you and Doreen, but they went straight to voicemail.

The next step was brave and, in hindsight, foolishly quixotic. Laying down an empty shopping bag on its side and holding it open like a cat flap, I pleaded with Sonny to get in. Passers-by looked on with amusement. Some even rolled their eyes but didn't interfere. They probably thought it was a matter best left between a man and his cat. Sonny gave me a look like I had never had from anyone, let alone a cat. It was one of undisguised contempt and disdain, roughly translating to,

"Are you real?"

Thinking about it now, there was no way any cat would have willingly walked into a bag. But at the time, it seemed a good idea. I inched the bag closer, mentally assessing the risk of my intended actions. Having been immunised against rabies after a recent stray dog bite abroad, I felt quite sanguine about a potential animal attack. Just then, an approaching dog barked, and Sonny, who I thought was nearly in the bag, bolted. I ran after him, bag in hand.

"Sonny, Sonny, stop! Please."

Finding him behind a bush in Monks Brook, I walked onto the precarious-looking bridge. Whipping out my phone, I called our mutual neighbour Angela and switched to video mode. She confirmed it was indeed Sonny. She agreed to knock on your door and alert you that your dear pet was hiding in the brook, half a mile away.

Meanwhile, I decided to hold Sonny's attention and not let him out of sight. Angela's call was due any minute. Whistling, meowing in several different tones – 'Meeeow,' 'Meooow,' 'Meowww' – and chanting the magic words 'Food, Food' in the exact intonation you had demonstrated, I balanced dangerously on the bridge. Sonny wasn't having any of it and stayed well away. This continued for a few minutes as I stood there, waiting for someone to call me and resolve the situation.

There we were – man and animal – locked in an endless stare-down: the benevolent rescuer of a lost pet, and a cat minding his own business until I came along.

My phone started playing Jimi Hendrix, and almost instinctively, I repositioned my headphones over my ears without losing eye contact with Sonny. I continued my meowing and cajoling, not realising that I was compensating for the volume of Hendrix's guitar. I was shouting. A small crowd began to gather, seeing this man with a black hoodie and an unruly beard imitating a cat at full throttle while balanced on a dodgy plank across the brook. It didn't help that they couldn't see the cat.

The expected phone call never came. Sonny, bored with the staring game, leapt across and disappeared into the industrial estate on the other side of the brook. After some feeble attempts to follow him, I gave up on the rescue mission. I felt for you and Doreen while continuing the evening walk, burdened with guilt and disappointment. In my mind, I was already helping you post notices about your missing cat.

Looking at the phone on reaching home, I saw two missed calls and a message from Angela: 'Paul's cat's asleep on his sofa. Enjoy your walk!'

Please warn Sonny – there is an impostor about.

~

103

Rory and Me

My life was turned upside down by a Bengal tiger. In December 2000, my friend Danny and I took a gap year after school to travel the world. The University of Edinburgh had made me a firm offer to study veterinary science the following year. Life seemed sorted, or so I imagined.

We travelled to Burma just after Christmas that year. A month later, we parted ways. I travelled to Malaysia. My funds soon started drying up, but fortunately, I found a temporary job at Negara Zoo, 15 miles from Kuala Lumpur.

The job role was advertised as 'Zoo Assistant'. No one told me it was a euphemism for 'Zoo Gopher'. There were some decent perks though: free accommodation in the wardens' quarters and access to subsidised meals in the staff canteen. My working day was spent among exotic animals. The welcoming Malay people, delightfully fresh cuisine, and warm tropical weather were reason enough for me to prolong my stay.

The animals lived in enclosures that simulated their natural habitat. Several CCTV cameras monitored their behaviour, and the zoo's vet attended to any that looked unwell. Somewhere along the way, my job role changed. Gradually, I stopped running errands and found myself accompanying the vet wherever she went. My colleagues called me *Adik* or younger brother.

The months that followed were spent learning about the ailments and quirks of animals. I felt privileged. A university course couldn’t have given me such practical experience.

“Adik, today we will check Sara's eyes,” the vet would typically announce when I reported for work. Sara was the hippopotamus. Ali, the macaque; Abdul and Noor, the elephants; Fatima, the orangutan: we were like a big and diverse family.

“Puteri is pregnant,” the vet told me one morning.

Puteri was the much-loved Bengal tigress.

“I'm not looking forward to it Adik. She's miscarried twice.”

I checked on the tigress several times during the day and spent my free time researching the care of newly born tiger cubs. My life at the zoo was blissful contentment.

There was, however, a thorn in my side: the gun-toting security guard, Umar. I knew he was trouble from the moment I saw him. His beady eyes set close together like the headlights of an old jeep, heralded my undoing.

Umar followed me everywhere. When the vet and I entered an enclosure, he cocked his rifle and stood ready. He didn't share my sense of camaraderie with the animals and saw them as wild creatures who would devour him given an opportunity. He treated them with disdain, referring to them as *binatang* or beasts.

“Look Umar,” I tried reasoning with him. “Wild animals don't attack unless provoked.”

“No, no, Adik. Binatangs dangerous. Western peoples much stupid,” he admonished me in his limited English.

Pointing to his right temple, he made tight circles with his index finger. In his estimation, I was both stupid and crazy!

One of Umar's favourite stories was that of the lion who asked a cat to teach him everything he knew. Apparently, the cat complied but didn't teach him how to climb trees. Thinking that he had learned everything, the lion, true to his mean nature, decided to kill the cat and gave chase. The cat climbed the nearest tree and saved himself.

"Never trust a Binatang," he underlined the moral of his story, wagging his rifle under my nose, breathing raw onions on my face.

13 May 2001: my nineteenth birthday.

I woke early to check on the heavily pregnant Puteri. In the dim light of dawn, I saw her lying motionless under a tree. I ran into her enclosure. Curled up next to her lifeless body was her new-born cub not yet strong enough to stand or open its eyes. It was a ball of yellow-orange and black fur, tiniest of paws and tail, candyfloss tongue.

The muezzin's call from a faraway mosque sounded like an elegy to mark the passing of dear Puteri. The early morning chorus of tropical birds welcomed the new-born. It was as if life and death were squaring up to each other in that brief twilight moment. The cub whimpered, tremulously seeking its dead mother's teats.

"You take charge of the cub, Adik," said the vet, struggling to hide her tears.

I named him Rory. I was his surrogate mother, bottle feeding him milk fortified with vitamins, playing with him and sometimes even sneaking him up to my room. He grew rapidly and within weeks was bounding about like a playful kitten.

Rory's enclosure was nearly an acre and the flora of the rainforest made it appear even larger. Teak and ebony trees canopied the skies. The scent of wild orchids wafted through the air and evanescent rainbows danced in the mid-morning light as the swift stream splashed against boulders. Bottle green frogs with bloodshot eyes croaked.

Five years passed. The England I left behind was a fading memory. I had lost my place at the University. But I didn't care. Rory had grown into a fully mature animal almost six feet long, not including the tail. His roar reverberated in the vast open spaces of the zoo, stopping both visitors and staff in their tracks. But he was a gentle, beautiful giant with his velvet coat and marble eyes. I spent most of my leisure time with him, swimming in the stream, tumbling in the tall grass and mock-fighting. In the summer, Rory liked to doze on a flat granite rock by the stream, near the bamboo bush.

Umar hadn't changed. After twenty years of employment in the zoo, he hadn't developed any empathy for its animals. His rifle always cocked and ready, he constantly tapped the trigger with his index finger. We hardly spoke to each other, but he never let me out of his sight, shadowing me as if he were my personal bodyguard.

21 June 2006, 6 p.m: I was at the far end of the enclosure under the mango tree. Rory was dozing on his favourite rock just outside the cave at the opposite end. His shining coat of tan and black merged with the yellow trunks of the bamboo trees as the light of the late afternoon sun cast its long shadows. Stretched languidly on that rock, his belly heaving gently with every breath, he was a poster for serenity.

My memory of what happened next plays out in slow

motion, as if my brain struggles to cope with the speed of the event.

Rory abruptly stood up from his rock and looked in my direction as if he was puzzled by something he had seen. Every sinew on his body was taut. His long tail went straight and rigid. His powerful forepaws were tensed and arched slightly forward. With whiskers twitching slightly and eyes narrowed to a slit, he looked straight at me. He was a statue. Umar, with the keenness of a hunter about to claim his first trophy, watched him intensely. His rifle was pointed directly at Rory through the gap in the steel fence.

Rory leapt off the rock, charged forward, and when he was a few feet away, lunged in my direction. I had never seen him move so quickly. I stood paralysed, arms across my face, and body twisted in fear. A single gunshot. A thousand surprised birds took flight. Rory, suspended mid-air for a microsecond, fell in a heap at my feet. Twitching three or four times, he became still.

Umar ran in and dragged me out of the enclosure. On the way out, he emptied his rifle into Rory's inert body. A mixture of emotions drove my tears as a chasm opened within. An overwhelming sense of loss – friendship, trust, innocence – engulfed me. Rory's betrayal broke me and I wailed like a child.

Overnight, Umar became a national hero and was awarded the JPP medal, Malaysia's highest honour for bravery in civilian life. The image of Rory's lifeless body was splashed across every newspaper in the country. TV channels broadcast the CCTV footage in a sequence of grainy black and white images. Rory leaping in the air towards me; I, cowering in the corner with my arms shielding my face; Umar pulling the trigger, and

Rory's lifeless body. The sequence played continuously, in a torturous loop.

I took the next flight home. The experience of having been proven naive and stupid, just as Umar had characterised me, left a festering wound on my personality. I became suspicious of people's motives and my acerbic cynicism cost me the few friends that I had. Moving from job to job, finding comfort in drink, I was a walking wreck.

One evening, my phone rang. People rarely called me. It was an unknown number, but I answered.

"Hello mate. It's Danny. Remember me? Danny McPherson?"

His voice smashed through the floodgate of memories that I had locked away and hoped to forget in time. I had to stop and lean against a lamppost. The demons of my past were out once again, ready to torment me.

Wondering how he had managed to trace me, I struggled to sound pleased.

"Hello Danny! It's so nice to hear from you. Been so long."

We agreed to meet at the weekend in Edinburgh, where he ran a successful multimedia business. He had watched the Rory incident on YouTube.

"Oh boy! Weren't you lucky! The gunshot really got two birds, didn't it?" Danny said.

I didn't understand him and looked at him in confusion.

"What two birds?"

"You mean you didn't know?" It was Danny's turn to be puzzled.

He played the CCTV footage on a giant screen. He paused at the point when Umar shoots Rory and stepped through the video, frame by frame. A flurry of birds takes to the air. He zoomed in just around my legs. A cobra, mostly hidden by the grass and inches away from me, quickly lowers its hood and disappears into the bushes.

~

104

The Last Light

Vishu[13] is the day when I wake up too early but dare not open my eyes. It is torment waiting for mother to lead me to the first sight of the year – the *Vishukkani*. I know that forbearance must prevail over my youthful impatience – I must wait for the auspicious moment. I hear her opening my door and shut my eyes even tighter. It hurts.

Her left hand gently covers my eyes, and her right guides me by the shoulder. We walk carefully down the stairs and into the *puja* room, where, working late into the night, she has laid out the Vishukkani. She seats me on a low stool draped in white and slips away, instructing me to keep my eyes shut until she leaves. I am already imagining the next event – lighting the firecrackers, roasted to perfection in the sun. I have no reason to think this Vishu will be any different from the others.

On mother's command, I open my eyes. I see my reflection in a large mirror. Its edges are decorated with sandalwood paste. The light from the coconut oil lamps illuminates the room. My New Year opens with sights of plenitude all around me. The mirror doubles the effect.

Navadhanya – nine types of grains, *Panchaloha* – five base metals, betel nuts, split coconuts, golden cucumbers and other vegetables, seasonal fruits, blood-red hibiscus and

---

13 *Vishu, a traditional festival celebrated by the people of Kerala and marks the beginning of the Malayalam New Year.*

fragrant jasmine. Maha Vishnu, the creator, is resting on his serpent; Mahalakshmi, goddess of wealth, is showering gold with two hands while twirling lotus flowers with the other two; and Saraswati, goddess of knowledge, is playing the lute. They smile beatifically down at me from the walls.

A large *uruli* contains uncooked rice, and incense sticks impaled on tiny yellow bananas fill the room with fragrant smoke. A fire-hardened clay pot is full of sweet *neyyappam*, and I eat as many as I want – the only day I am allowed to eat in the morning before brushing my teeth. The smell of jasmine melds with those of sandalwood and hot coconut oil. It lingers.

I feel the softness of my mother's feet as I touch them to receive her blessings and the usual gift of one silver rupee. Father too gives me a rupee, as do my older siblings.

Dawn breaks. The neighbourhood erupts in celebration, and the sky is painted with rainbow flares; the smell of sulphur and whistling flowerpots frame the scene. The joy is almost palpable. Adults sip tea and watch us as we revel in the best festival of the year.

"Careful!" they exhort us, but we pay no heed. I race around with my siblings and cousins, live sparklers in our hands and our mouths stuffed with neyyappam. Then, suddenly, a stray spark lands on our stock of fireworks. There's a hiss, then a crackle.

For a heartbeat, nothing happens. Then – pandemonium.

The spectacle in the sky descends into our veranda. It is as if a pack of snarling beasts has been unleashed among us. Crazed rockets ricochet off the walls. Catherine wheels whip and spin around my legs. Cascades of furious explosions deafen me, and my ears ring. Dazzling brilliance engulfs the chaos.

A rocket in full flight slams into the bridge of my nose – and explodes. Pain sears through my burning face. My eyes squeeze shut. When I open them again, the world is gone. I cannot hear my own screams of pain and panic. The din is unrelenting.

I am left with memories nearly as vivid as sight: Vishukkani, mother's smiling face, and a joyous childhood. The fragrance of the day lingers – jasmine, hot coconut oil, sandalwood. Fireworks too.

~

105

Khuda Hafiz: Encounters with Humanity

In Bangalore airport, a small boy ran headlong into me, almost throwing me off balance. His mother, clad in a black burqa, came up and apologised profusely. She spoke fluent English and gently prompted the boy to say 'sorry.' I was taken aback – not by the apology, but by how misplaced my own assumptions had been. I had never spoken to someone in a burqa before. Somewhere along the way, I had absorbed the foolish idea that someone in a burqa would likely be uneducated and unable to communicate. That moment exposed the narrowness of my thinking.

Later that day, on the flight from Bangalore to Dubai, I found myself seated next to a young lad. I had the aisle seat; he was in the middle, and a white man sat at the window. The boy leaned heavily against me, his weight awkwardly shifting into my side. I was growing irritated, though I kept quiet.

As we waited for take-off, he received a phone call. From the affectionate way he spoke to his parents and the words he used, I realised he was a Muslim. His voice trembled as he ended the call with 'Khuda Hafiz.' Something in me softened.

I figured that if I started a conversation, he'd have to sit up and respond – which might relieve my squashed shoulder too. I began speaking with him. As expected, he shifted to the centre of his seat and answered politely. He was on his way to Riyadh, where he worked as a marketing assistant. I asked if he had done the Hajj, and he said he was hoping to go soon, with his parents.

As we talked, I asked whether he felt discriminated against in India because of his faith. He paused, then answered with a wisdom beyond his years: yes, sometimes. But most people were good to him, most of the time. That, he said, was true everywhere. Good and bad people exist in all places – but mostly, people are good. He spoke bitterly of the terrorists who had hijacked Islam and expressed hope that people would learn to tell the difference.

We parted in Dubai with a warm "Khuda Hafiz."

On the second leg of my journey – from Dubai to London – I watched *The Idol*, a biopic about Mohammed Assaf, the legendary singer from Gaza who gave hope to millions in the Middle East through his music. It was refreshing to see how the human spirit persists despite every hardship. The film offered a glimpse into daily life in Gaza – not headlines or horror, but children, families, neighbours. It was sobering and deeply human.

Each time I return to India, I sense a growing hostility toward Muslims. Sparse interaction between communities has made it difficult for people to distinguish between extremists and the average Muslim. The actions of a violent minority are used to stereotype an entire community.

The solution, I believe, lies in human contact. We must go beyond surface impressions, beyond clothing and culture, and make real connections. Only then can we begin to dismantle the harmful generalisations that drive division.

There are no good terrorists or bad terrorists. But there are good Muslims and bad Muslims – just as there are good and bad people in every group. Our task is not to reject an entire community, but to isolate the extremists by standing shoulder to shoulder with those who are peaceful.

Like the wise lad on the plane reminded me: most people are good, most of the time.

If we truly believe that, then we must begin by reaching out – not with suspicion, but with trust in our shared humanity.

~

106

Warning Bells from the Future

'Once this is all over,' claimed an optimistic newspaper article, "the world will be a better place." Perhaps. However, this depends largely on the lessons we learn during this crisis.

Have we learned that our happiness is not enhanced by the possessions that surround us, but by learning to do without them? Have we realised that we need not jump on the next plane to the remotest corner of the planet simply because we have convinced ourselves that the further we travel, the better the holiday? Have we understood that many meetings for minor decisions need not require travel across the country or the world, but can be conducted just as efficiently from our desks, at home or at work?

Will we recognise, in retrospect, when this is all over, that the old normality – in which we took things for granted – is no longer tenable? That when communities are devastated by floods and bushfires, we too bear some indirect responsibility? Will we continue to be helpless while unnecessary wars decimate ancient civilisations, driving people to starvation and destitution? Now that we share even a diluted and well-managed glimpse of their misery, will we begin to consider what we could do as individuals? Have we learned to connect ourselves with those less fortunate, and to link our insatiable desires with the degradation of the planet that sustains us?

Or will we simply revert to our profligate, wasteful ways

and carry on as if nothing happened? Will we learn these lessons now – to turn off the tap while washing our hands for 20 seconds, to sustain the new-found camaraderie with our neighbours rather than retreating into our shells, to reject imported apples from New Zealand or avocados from Chile in favour of local produce, and to reconsider our work habits, avoiding printing reams of paper when we could simply read documents onscreen? Or are we going to forget everything and revert to our old ways?

What we are experiencing now is but a small taster of things to come – a warning bell from the future. It is up to us to decide how our future, and that of generations to come, will unfold.

~

107

British Etiquette

(An abridged version of this, 'Fawlty Manners', was published by The Times of India on 24 September 2024)

Robert Burns, the famous Scottish poet once wrote 'A Man's a Man for A' That.' My advice to you therefore is – be yourself and you will be fine. However, since you ask, I will jot down some thoughts accumulated over three decades on this island.

While here, lubricate your sentences with a liberal dose of the favourite British words 'thank you' and 'sorry'. It is your fault if you bang into someone. It is still your fault if someone bangs into you – say sorry promptly. The only exception is when you are involved in a motoring accident – when you never say sorry because if you do, you would be accepting liability. The other party's insurance company will take you to the cleaners.

Don't spit on the road. In fact, refrain from spitting in the sink (wash basin) of a public toilet. Definitely, don't blow your nose or gargle into the sink. If you must clean out your mouth after a meal, use a toothbrush. However, you could be mistaken for a vagrant if you are unlucky. Use a tissue or a handkerchief to blow your nose. Once used, delicately deposit it in your pocket.

You will see some youth in large cities vomiting and urinating on a Friday night after a few too many pints on a night out. Don't emulate them. As a general rule, do not litter. Carry your rubbish with you until you find a litter bin. However, don't deposit your litter in a wheelie bin on the kerb. Don't ask me why, but people get very upset if you do.

If you are seeking clarification on any point, do not ask the same question of several people; be discreet if you must. Do not make unnecessary eye contact with people. If you do, either wish them good morning/afternoon/evening or just smile. Careful with younger people, though. To them, say Hi or Hello. While most young people are friendly, some can be unruly, so approach with caution.

Elderly/middle-aged people are the safest among strangers to ask for directions. Never jump queues and never ask anyone if you can get to the front of one. Do not cling to the person in front of you in a queue; maintaining such physical contact with strangers will mark you out as a perv. Do not show any affection to children other than your own. Pat them tenderly and you are a paedo; smack a feral, uncontrollable monster and you will be had for assault on a minor.

Shake hands when introduced to people. You may see some people doing a cheek-to-cheek air kiss with those of the opposite sex – this is only for those who know each other. When you part company with someone, don't shake hands repeatedly and say 'bye' several times. Don't linger, just go.

Do not turn up unannounced at anyone's residence. If invited to someone's house for a meal, always carry a bottle of wine and flowers if a woman is involved. Offer to remove your shoes upon entering their home. Your coat will normally be taken by your host, to be returned intact when you depart. This is also common practice in good restaurants; don't leave wallets and phones in the coat. It is considered rude if you don't buy a round of drinks at the bar. You need your wallet more than the impoverished waiter who stored your coat.

If you go to a shop, wait for your turn to be served. The shopkeeper and his customer will react as if you have insulted their mothers if you butt in. Shopkeepers don't multitask. If you cannot wait for your turn, say why you are butting in – try, 'I am sorry to interrupt, but my train is about to leave and...'

Don't talk over others in meetings; never point at people and refer to them as 'he' or 'she', but always take their name. So, don't say, 'As he said ...', but say, 'As Mike/Mary said ...'. If you don't remember their name, say, 'I am sorry, but I forget your name.' Even if the person is sitting next to you, the use of the third-person pronoun is proscribed. The use of first names is not considered rude or overly familiar behaviour. As a rule of thumb, except for the very first time, address people by their first name always.

If you pass through a door, keep the door open for the next person. No harm in holding it open and waiting for someone to catch up. Don't overdo it, or else they will think you have lost it. Do not stare at people and do not join in random conversations just because you know the right answer. Minding one's own business is up there with cleanliness in its proximity to God.

While travelling, do not ask to borrow newspapers or magazines from fellow passengers. Don't even think about pulling out the middle page of the newspaper just because its owner may still be reading the front page.

Don't get carried away when people say 'Brilliant', 'Excellent', 'You are a star' and so on. England is a country of superlatives. However, beware of the prefix 'not', especially the 'not brilliant' expression, which basically means 'rubbish' and not one grade below brilliant. Beware of the general propensity to indulge in role-playing. When someone says, 'I wouldn't do it if I were you', don't be perplexed. They just mean, 'Don't do it'.

The term 'plebs' is used by some English snobs, but it is best avoided.

Do not participate in jokes about gays, lesbians, transgenders, transsexuals, Irish, black and ethnic minorities, the elderly, or any minority group for that matter. Don't discuss religion or politics with casual acquaintances.

You will hear many new expressions, half of which you will not understand. Keeping a steady smile on your face can mask your incomprehension. Expressions such as 'last but not least', 'Tom, Dick and Harry', and 'wild goose chase' are last-century speak. Avoid them. Keep your ears open for some very creative and apt expressions.

'Prepone' is not standard English, and 'thrice' is rarely used outside of old literature. Note the perennial confusion between 'meantime' and 'meanwhile'. 'In the meantime' is correct, while 'in the meanwhile' is wrong. Do not refer to your son as 'my kid' unless you want them to think you are talking about your pet goat.

What else? Keep your sense of humour about you. All transgressions of common etiquette are forgiven if you know how to laugh, even when the joke is on you. Remember, Albert Camus said, 'Human beings are the most absurd of God's creations.' Etiquette is the creation of human beings.

~

108

Football Didn't Come Home

Perhaps this is as good a time as any to debate the most difficult question of all: are we, longstanding immigrants to this country, British? Not just the holder of a British passport, but in how we genuinely feel? Do we feel part of the milieu of multicultural Britain or are we full of resentment towards a society that we perceive to have excluded us? Where do we stand?

As far as I am concerned, I fail the Tebbit test every time India plays cricket against England. I unequivocally support India and want them to win. Every time – without exception. When I got sucked into the national football fever that had gripped England in recent months, I felt English, completely and without conflict. I wanted England to win even though a part of me abhorred the gladiatorial fervour of the braying crowds. Nevertheless, I sat at home in my comfortable leather chair and cheered England with a beer in hand. And I liked the feeling. Football is coming home, I too chanted, suspending self-flagellating doubts. Don't analyse an ice cream, I said to myself – just enjoy it while it lasts.

Then I thought again of the Tebbit test, and my brain went into a tizzy considering the hypothetical and dangerously existentialist conundrum – what if India was playing England in football? Who would I support? I had no answer – I could not, hand on heart, say I would support one or the other. I let that question ferment in my head. Quite fortuitously, I remembered the words of the Nobel Prize-winning economist Amartya Sen – paraphrased – one can have multiple identities; there is no need to swear allegiance to anything.

So, I concluded, I support England in football and India in cricket. I am all of British, English, and Indian – that sequence in alphabetical order. I have multiple identities and therefore, multiple allegiances. And perhaps none. It is my prerogative to make that choice, or not.

I hear you ask: what about all the hidden racism that we suffer in this country? The missed promotions, the absent nods and winks, the conversations where people don't make eye contact, the projects that were not given to me even though I was eminently qualified? Yes, what about those? I have no answer – I have concluded that perhaps I was not the most qualified to be 'picked', perhaps there were subtle things I didn't know – things I shouldn't have said – things that I didn't imbibe as my upbringing was different, my cultural inheritance made of different stuff – or even more brutally – maybe I wasn't just competent enough. I don't know, and I don't think I ever will. It gives me comfort to leave it at that.

That for every bigot who cannot make eye contact with me or carry on a normal conversation with me because of how I look and how I talk, I have met a hundred others who are happy to engage with me and value my friendship. They appreciate me for what I am, not for what I ought to be. They let me be me.

So, I am English – but not the English who break bottles and piss on the streets – but the overwhelming majority of others who are polite, kind and considerate – those who don't interfere with me or my family on the streets, those who know how to respect my privacy and leave me alone, but those who will leap at the first opportunity to help me – if I ask for help.

Football didn't come home, I did.

~

Acknowledgements

Jan Hawes, my editor, close friend, and ex-colleague: I am deeply grateful and indebted to you for reading every word, and editing with care, always keeping my voice and rhythm intact. Thank you for making only minimal changes to the style and mechanics of the text. You stood by me throughout the publishing process, always offering sane counsel. Without your help, I would have struggled to present a polished version. I must also thank my publisher for their meticulous and artistic work.

Many friends, especially the alumni of DMET, the marine engineering academy where I studied, have been suggesting that I publish a collection of my stories. A big thank you to all of you. You are too numerous to name.

A note of thanks to Geoff Parkes, my writing friend and grammarian, who never turned down a request to review some of my newspaper stories or clarify a point of language. I am also grateful to my extended family, both the OC and KT clans, and my son Siddharth for all their support and encouragement.

Sujata, my wife and the love of my life: without mincing words or sugarcoating them, you told me exactly what you thought as I passed each story by you. You did not resort to euphemisms in your criticism but always gave me your considered opinion on everything. I always took your suggestions seriously, although I sometimes bristled at your forthrightness. Deep inside, I valued your judgement over my own.

About The Author

Gopi (Gopinath Chandroth, formerly O. C. Gopinath) is, by training, a marine engineer, having graduated from the Directorate of Marine Engineering Training, India, in 1978. He has over four decades of experience in the shipping industry, the first fifteen years spent on merchant ships. Before settling ashore, he obtained a Master of Science in Software Engineering and a doctorate in Artificial Intelligence for machinery condition monitoring from the University of Sheffield, UK. The last fifteen years of his career were spent working for the UK Government's Marine Accident Investigation Branch as an Inspector of Marine Accidents.

He writes purely for fun and has been published in leading newspapers such as The Times of India and Deccan Herald. He has also contributed to several anthologies of short stories. He currently lives in the UK and shares his writings on his blog at www.gopistory.com. He can be contacted by email: gopinath.chandroth@gmail.com